Guide to Quality Control

Dr Kaoru Ishikawa

Asian Productivity Organization

TOKYO

Guide to Quality Control

Dr Kaoru Ishikawa

Second Revised Edition

Asian Productivity Organization

Available in North America,
the United Kingdom and Western Europe
exclusively from:
UNIPUB
Box 433 Murray Hill Station
New York, N.Y. 10157, U.S.A.
Tel. No. (800)521-8110

Some other titles published by the ASIAN PRODUCTIVITY ORGANIZATION
- Quality Control Circles at Work
- Modern Production Management
- Bases for Science and Technology Promotion in Developing Countries
- Japan's Quality Control Circle
- Technoeconomics – Concepts and Cases
- Japanese-style Management: Its Foundations and Prospects
- Organizing for Higher Productivity: An Analysis of Japanese Systems and Practices
- Profitability Analysis for Managerial and Engineering Decisions
- Management by Objectives: A Japanese Experience
- How to Measure Maintenance Performance
- Measuring and Enhancing the Productivity of Service and Government Organization
- Preparing for Standardization, Certification and Quality Control
- Productivity Through Consultancy in Small Industrial Enterprises
- Guidelines for Management Consultants in Asia
- 100 Management Charts
- Preparing Feasibility Studies in Asia

Designed and Printed in Hong Kong by
NORDICA INTERNATIONAL LIMITED
for
ASIAN PRODUCTIVITY ORGANIZATION
4-14, Akasaka 8-chome
Minato-ku, Tokyo 107, Japan

ISBN 92-833-1035-7 (Casebound)
ISBN 92-833-1036-5 (Limpbound)

GEMBA NO QC SHUHO (in Japanese)
by K. Ishikawa (ed.)
Copyright 1968 by JUSE Press Ltd., Tokyo
Translated into English by the
Asian Productivity Organization

First Published 1972
First Revised Edition 1976
Second Revised Edition 1982
Fifteenth Printing (with amendments and index) February 1985

Contents

Preface to the Second Revised English Edition

Following publication of the revised edition of "Guide to Quality Control" in 1976, the book soon came to be regarded as the best book on quality control as practised in Japan. Five reprints have since been made, and large companies in the United States have used the book as an indispensable part of their in-house training kit.

On the basis of the feedback from actual application of the techniques discussed in the book, Dr. Kaoru Ishikawa, the author, has made improvements in a number of graphs in chapters 2, 5 and 13. The improvements mainly concern the Pareto diagram and practice problems, making the quality control methodology more effective.

The Asian Productivity Organization (APO) is pleased to bring out this second revised edition and is confident that it will lead to further dissemination of quality control techniques which are essential to productivity improvement.

Tokyo, Japan
July, 1982

Asian Productivity Organization

Preface to the revised English edition

The Asian Productivity Organization published in April 1971 an English translation of the Japanese book "Genba no QC Shuho". Edited by Dr. Kaoru Ishikawa and published by the Japan Union of Scientists and Engineers, the book was written to introduce quality control practices in Japan which had contributed tremendously to the country's economy and industrial development. The translation was well received and stocks were exhausted shortly after publication.

It was therefore decided to bring out a new English version to meet the need for such a unique book with Asian characteristics applicable and adaptable to developing countries. In the course of preparing for a new edition, many shortcomings in the first translated version surfaced. They were due in part to the subtlety of the Japanese language and ambiguities in terminology, but mostly to practical difficulties in faithfully translating one language to another. The APO consulted Dr. Ishikawa on the matter and he was able to give valuable advice on how to revise the English version. Then the whole process of re-translation was launched with a team of translators working side by side with the APO's own staff; they had the guidance and technical advice of Prof. Norio Shibata of the Graduate School of Business Administration of the Keio University, Tokyo. The re-translation and careful review and checking took over a year to complete. This revised edition is, therefore, a new version entirely and is free of the shortcomings of the first one.

The book is intended as a guide rather than a detailed handbook. Those interested in further studying the subject of quality control should refer to other publications, some of which are listed in the bibliography at the end of this book. During the course of editing the new English translation, it was found necessary to include as appendices some additional material not included in the first edition or in the original Japanese version. A few footnotes were also added. Readers may now refer to these appendices and footnotes to obtain a better grasp of the contents, especially with regard to those chapters which are unique Japanese innovations, such as the chapter on a binomial probability paper. Also, "How to Use This Book" has been newly translated and inserted before the main body of the book.

The present book is suitable for both self-study and classroom training. As the quality control circle is a unique feature in Japan where workers study and analyze the quality control process on their own initiative, the original Japanese book served and is still serving the needs of QC circle members in their quest for improvement through group study and discussions. It would be ideal if national productivity organisations in APO member countries could encourage the use of this book in a similar manner for the benefit of foremen and workers to achieve even greater results.

The Asian Productivity Organization wishes to thank Prof. Kaoru Ishikawa and the Japan Union of Scientists and Engineers for their cooperation. It also wishes to thank Prof. N. Shibata, Interlingua Language Services Ltd, and all those who contributed towards this revised version.

Tokyo, February, 1976
ASIAN PRODUCTIVITY ORGANIZATION

Preface to the original edition

Japan's industrial workers are, qualitatively, among the world's finest. But further polishing is necessary for them to display their true brilliance and strength. Therefore, one of our aims in publishing *Quality Control for the Foreman* magazine and in starting the QC Circle activities was to enable workers to study together. Since then the QC Circle movement has become national, and it is now the object of world-wide attention.

Throughout Japan it is apparent that factory workers have the desire to study. Not only foremen but workers have begun reading about quality control and other subjects related to their work. The circulation of *Quality Control for the Foreman* has been rapidly increasing each month, and many books of the "factory QC reader" type are being published. We are pleased to see this trend.

To promote the desire to study, in 1968 we adopted the slogan: "QC Circle members — Let's study!" But in order to study, a proper textbook is necessary. And when that textbook has to serve millions of factory workers, it was apparent that those already published on QC were somewhat too sophisticated. Foremen also found these books inappropriate for training new employees. The result was a growing demand for an easier book.

This book builds upon the articles and exercises concerning QC which the Editorial Committee of *Quality Control for the Foreman* originally wrote for the magazine.

The techniques in this book are those we feel should be known by all QC Circle leaders and, if possible, all circle members as well. This book can be used for self study, training of employees by foremen, or in QC reading circles. However, this book contains only the techniques and is not concerned with the concept of QC, or the reasons behind it. Other books are available concerning those matters, and some of them are presented at the end of this book.*

As we compiled this book in haste, there may be some inadequacies. But we believe it was very useful to bring this information together in one volume. Reading the book should be helpful, though study alone is not enough. Techniques must be practised on the job!

I wish to thank Mr. Koichi Ohba for his help in publishing this book, and also the editorial staff of the JUSE Publishing Company.

April 1968   KAORU ISHIKAWA
                                                          Editorial Committee Chairman

---

*List of books in Japanese not included in this translated version

How to use this book

Study Method —

The explanations of QC techniques and the practice problems which appeared in the magazine *Quality Control at the Factory* during 1967 have been brought together in this book. To compile these chapters, which cover a year's publication of the magazine, studies on the fundamental techniques of quality control were made at the factories, and by the editing committee of the QC magazine. Thus the contents are something each factory foreman, group leader and circle leader should completely master. The question now is: how can you pursue your study most effectively?

Because of its origins, this book is not like an ordinary textbook; rather it is highly suitable for self-study. If you read the book carefully from cover to cover, you will naturally obtain a good understanding of the subject. However, let us guide you towards an effective study method so that you can attain full understanding and quality control can be of practical help. The following section will give you some hints on how to carry out your studies.

For those who wish to study on their own

Chapters 1 to 12 explain the techniques of quality control. Chapter 13, which embodies practice problems 1 to 12, provides practice problems and the answers. This final chapter also gives explanations that could not be covered fully in the first 12 chapters, especially additional explanations to help understand the answers to the practice problems. If you look at the table of contents, you will see that the numbers given to each chapter correspond to the numbers given to the practice problems in chapter 13.

For example, chapter 5 deals with Pareto diagrams, and practice problem 13.5 in the last chapter also deals with them.

When embarking on self-study, the following steps and tips will be helpful.

1. Read the explanations of QC techniques.
   - First, go over the whole chapter once. Even if you come across some parts that are not clear, keep on reading until the end of the chapter. In some cases, the parts you could not understand will be cleared up further on.
   - Once you have finished going over the whole chapter, go back to the beginning again, and read through leaving more time. Parts that are not clear should be read repeatedly until the contents are understood.
   - When going through the chapter for the second time, write down the words and formulas you think are important, as well as anything you did not understand, in a notebook.
   - After finishing the second reading, go over the words and formulas you have written in the notebook to see whether you really understand them. If you come across any you do not understand or are not certain of, read that part of the book again.
   - If you feel that you have "more or less understood" the contents, proceed to the next step. Even if you feel slightly uncertain about your comprehension, don't worry about carrying on as long as you have gone through the foregoing steps carefully.
2. Find the practice problems with the corresponding number and try to solve the problems.
   - Needless to say, don't refer to the answers from the beginning. If you have trouble solving them, go back to the chapter and read the contents again. Try to come up with some sort of answer.
   - Check your answer against the correct answer provided in the book.
   - Find out where the difference lies between your answer and the one in the book. Read the chapter once again, trying to discover the cause of the mistake, and try re-answering the problem.
   - If your answer corresponds to that in the book, congratulations! Carry on!
3. Read the explanations that follow the answers to the practice problems.
   - Here, you will come across new things that were not mentioned in the earlier chapters. So read this section carefully, in the same way as described in 1.
4. Once you've learned how to solve the practice problems, think about the data in your factory to which the techniques you have just studied

can be applied. You are bound to find such data if you look carefully enough. You may also come up with ideas on new types of data you want to collect.

5. If you can find data concerning matters you are already familiar with, try applying the techniques on the spot.

6. After applying them, show the result to the factory staff and your colleagues, and seek their criticism. It will be helpful if you ask their advice.

I am sure there will be cases where the example used in a given practice problem is not related to your kind of work. However, whether it has something to do with your field or not, you should be able to answer the problem if you have gone through the steps properly. Of course, self-study is hard and painstaking; the most important thing is to keep at it. If possible, it is advisable to form a study group with some of your friends.

For those who wish to study in a group

Group-study also involves a certain degree of self-study, since everyone is assigned problems to prepare, review and practise as homework. The way of going about this has been explained in the previous section. Here are some points that should be considered in group-study.

1. Study of the first 12 chapters (the explanations of the quality control techniques).
   - Everyone studies a bit on his own (self-study).
   - Take turns lecturing (rotating lecturer).
   - It is essential that those not appointed to lecture on a given topic should do the preparatory study work anyway.
   - Have someone from outside the group — for example, a helpful member of the factory staff who may be engaged in quality control activities — come and give lectures. The group members should prepare the lessons well and have questions ready.
   - Group members should exchange opinions in trying to find familiar problems to which the technique can be applied. Then they can discuss whether the application was suitable or not.

2. Practice problems. After finishing the study of the techniques, try solving the problems given for each technique (the practice problems in chapter 13 with the corresponding number).
   - Let each member of the group present his answer in turn. These answers should be written on a large sheet of paper beforehand, so they can be discussed among the members.
   - Do not be embarrassed about presenting your answer just because it might be wrong. The purpose is to discuss it with the others and use

it as material for study. It must be presented from the standpoint of "providing study material".

— The group should not only point out the mistakes but examine how to make improvements.
— When no conclusion can be reached even after discussion within the group, the group should read the chapter of the book together. If the problem is not solved at this stage, seek the cooperation of the staff members in the factory. But do not forget that the study must be accomplished by you, yourselves.
— The number of practice problems is limited. So, if you can find some similar data, try applying the techniques to the actual data. The results of this application should also be discussed by the group.

If these suggestions look helpful, take full advantage of them and study hard. You may face various obstacles, such as limited time, etc, but they can be overcome by active self-study. The foregoing steps may be rather strict but remember: slow but steady wins the race.

Chapter 1

How to collect data

1.1 The purpose of collecting data

A great deal of data are collected in factory situations. Let us first consider the purpose of collecting these data.

When we introduce a particular method of doing a job, it is natural that we consider whether the method is appropriate or not. The decision is usually based on past results and experience, or perhaps on conventional methods. However, in the case of factory work, where data are collected through the actual manufacturing process, the procedural methods are introduced on the basis of the information obtained. The manufacturing procedure will only be correct if a proper evaluation is made, and on-the-job data are essential for making a proper evaluation.

Since data will form the basis for action and decisions, the data which should be obtained from factory operations will vary with the manufacturing procedure involved. We have classified these data in terms of the various purposes.

(1) Data to assist in understanding the actual situation

These data are collected to check the extent of the dispersion in part sizes coming from the machining process, or to examine the percentage of defective parts contained in lots received. When the number of data increase, they can be arranged statistically for easier understanding, as will be explained further on. Estimates can then be made concerning the condition of lots received and the manufacturing process, through comparison with specified figures, standard figures, target figures, etc.

1

(2) Data for analysis

Analytical data may be used, for example, in examining the relationship between a defect and its cause. Data are collected by examining past results and making new tests. In this case, various statistical methods are used to obtain correct information.

(3) Data for process control

After investigating product quality, this kind of data can be used to determine whether or not the manufacturing process is normal. Control charts are used in this evaluation and action is taken on the basis of these data.

(4) Regulating data

This is the data used, for example, as the basis for raising or lowering the temperature of an electric furnace so that a standardized temperature level may be maintained. Actions are prescribed for each datum, and these measures must be taken accordingly.

(5) Acceptance or rejection data

This form of data is used for approving or rejecting parts and products after inspection. There are two methods — total inspection and sampling. On the basis of the information obtained, it can be decided what to do with the parts or products.

1.2 Correct data

As we have explained, data serve as the basis for action. After evaluating the actual conditions, as revealed by the data, the proper action can be taken. Thus, the most important thing to do first is to determine whether or not the data represent typical conditions. The problem can be stated as follows:

1) Will the data gathered reveal the facts?

2) Are the data collected, analyzed and compared in such a way as to reveal the facts?

No. 1 is a problem of sampling methods; No. 2 is a problem of statistical processing.

The most important point in sampling is to know just what the data are used for — in other words, to be certain of the purpose. For example, if the problem with a given product is impurity dispersion, it is hardly sufficient to take only one sample per day to find out the daily dispersion rate. Or, in comparing defects produced by workers A and B, it is essential to take two separate samples from both workers' products. It means one must give full consideration to the reason for collecting data, proper sampling techniques, and stratification. One should not take a disproportionate share of a certain kind of data simply because they can be collected easily. Also, partial data which happen to be convenient to collect are not necessarily effective data.

But even the use of proper sampling techniques is not enough. It is necessary to see that the data represent the facts and that the statistical method applied is such that an objective evaluation can be made.

For example, even if you have 100 data showing the hardness of material X, it is generally impossible to draw any conclusions from the numerical value alone. The basis for a decision can only be obtained after comparing them with the overall situation, as in a histogram or check sheet. And, in comparing the hardness of material Y with that of material X, it is still necessary to use statistical techniques, after considering the dispersion in the samples of each.

1.3 Kind of data

Now, even assuming that the need for having data is understood, there will still be some group leaders who say: "I can't find any data on my job," or "I can't collect data." Of course, on our jobs it is often hard to obtain data in neat numerical values. Whenever man tries to measure the softness of fabrics, plating lustre, or the whiteness of paper, neat numerical figures such as one encounters for size and weight are, naturally, impossible to obtain.

Let us suppose that you have to determine the softness of three kinds of fabric. Even if you cannot measure the exact softness, by arranging the fabrics in order of softness, you can obtain excellent data. The vibration of an automobile, or flickering during the projection of an 8mm motion picture, would be difficult to measure with simple instruments alone. But one can also have five persons test drive the car or watch the movies and then report their observations, and thus obtain good data.

As previously stated, the purpose of collecting data is not to put everything into neat figures but to provide a basis for action. The data can be in any form.

Generally, data can be divided into these groups:

    A. Measurement data: continuous data
           Length, weight, time, etc.

    B.   Countable data: enumerate data
         Number of defectives, number of defects, percentage defective, etc.

However, in addition to that there are also:

    C.   Data on relative merits
    D.   Data on sequences
    E.   Data on grade points

These data are used frequently by many factory and group leaders with long experience, who can draw appropriate conclusions from them.

1.4 Analysis of data

After data are collected, they are analyzed, and information is extracted through the use of statistical methods. Therefore, data should be collected in such a way as to simplify later analysis.

First of all, clearly record the nature of the data. If some time passes between the collection and the analysis of the data, no one might be able to remember where the data came from. There is a great deal of data in a factory, but they very often become dead data because their nature was not clearly recorded. It is necessary to record not only the purpose of the measurement and its characteristics but also the date, the instruments used, the person doing it, the method, and so on.

Next, record the data in such a way that they are easy to use. Since grand totals, averages, and ranges are often computed later, it is easier if the data are recorded with this in mind. If 100 data are taken at one time, any form of data sheet will probably do, but if one datum is taken five times a day at 9 am, 11 am, 1 pm, 3 pm and 5 pm, over a 20-day period, then the data sheet should show the time horizontally and the date vertically. If this is done, then the daily total can be made for each column and the hourly total for each line. The secret to successful analysis is to make skilful use of the data sheet, both vertically and horizontally. If you have readymade data sheets or check sheets in your factory, the above points have probably already been taken into consideration. However, it is always worthwhile to check again to ensure that the data can be collected easily and analyzed automatically.

1.5 Reminders for collecting data

Pay attention to the following points when collecting data:

(1) Remember to take action according to the data

We must always remember to make data the basis of our actions, otherwise they will not be collected in a positive manner. Get into the habit of discussing a problem on the basis of the data and respecting the facts as shown by them.

(2) Clarify the purpose of collecting the data

In addition to this, it is still necessary to make the purpose clear. Only then can the necessary comparisons and the kinds of data to be collected be determined. It is important to review the purpose of the data being collected and also to see if they are really being put to effective use.

(3) Remember to get everything into data

Just because the kind of data needed has been determined it does not automatically follow that such data can be collected. Lack of instruments or manpower, difficulties in quantification, etc, are common problems. What is essential at this stage is a will and ingenuity for collecting data. The key to the solution is whether one can collect data skilfully. The difference between good and poor factory and group leaders becomes evident here. The good leaders take great pains to obtain data and often come up with unique methods.

Chapter 2

Histograms

2.1 Data have dispersion

In Chapter 1 we studied how to collect data. Now let us consider how to arrange these data.

Every day in the factory we collect data in various forms. For example, we collect data on yield, percentage of defective items, operating rate, absenteeism, diameter of poles, solidity of wire, and weight or concentration of products, to record them in daily reports, graphs and control charts.

There is a purpose to collecting all these data. Try thinking about the reason behind the data you are collecting. Is the purpose clear? For example, let's suppose you have taken ten samples from a certain lot and have measured them. Using as our basis the data from these samples, which were chosen at random, we can make inferences about the measurement of articles from the entire lot from which these data were taken, or from the production process, and then take some kind of action (see figure 2.1).

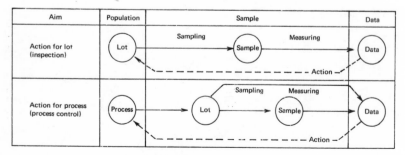

Figure 2.1 Population and sample

Data are required to obtain the average dimensions and the degree of dispersion so that we can determine whether it is alright to receive or ship the lot, and whether the production process used for manufacturing the lot was suitable, or if some action must be taken. *In other words, we are about to take action on a lot or process on the basis of data gained from the samples we have taken.*

Products from the same production line usually differ slightly in dimension, hardness or other qualities. If, after measuring ten samples, they were all found to measure 10.0, 10.0, 10.0 ... 10.0, there would be cause for doubt. We would suspect that the measuring instrument was wrong or we might even wonder if they had ever been measured at all! We commute to work every day and even if we take the same route and the same vehicle we usually find that on some days the trip doesn't take as long as others. If we tried to make the trip in exactly the same time every day, it would require a good deal of effort. In this way, when we look at a certain amount of data we can detect some dispersion. Actually, we live in a *world of dispersion*. To know the quality of a given amount of products, we must use averages and dispersion.

Take, for example, the life of an electrical appliance. Even if, on the average, the 'life' of the appliance is long, if there is much dispersion some of the appliances will wear out rapidly. This implies a loss in reliability of the product. That means one criterion for judging the quality of products is whether, on the average, the life is long and at the same time the dispersion is small.

Let's assume that we take four samples of a certain part from the production line daily for one month and take measurements. There are two ways of looking at the data for the 100 samples:

 1)   Overall appearance of the parts as a group.
 2)   Changes in the daily measurements over one month.

For (1), we can construct a frequency table showing the number of parts for each dimension. Then, if we make a histogram, it will be easy to find the shape, the central value, and the manner of dispersion of the size measurement. For (2), in order to see the changes in the data chronologically, control charts or graphs giving the date vertically and the dimensions horizontally are often used. Let us take case (1) and see how to construct and use a histogram.

2.2 How to prepare a histogram

The data in table 2.1 represent the thickness (in millimetres) of 100 metal blocks that are parts of optical instruments. When there is as much

7

data as the 100 samples here, it is difficult to determine the distribution of data just by looking at the figures. In a situation such as this, if we arrange the data in sequence orders and show how many figures are alike (see table 2.1), and then draw up a graph, we can perceive the overall tendency. There are many kinds of graphs, but one of the most common is the *histogram* (figure 2.2). Let's examine the method for making a histogram.

(1) Count the data. $N = 100$

(2) As shown in table 2.1, divide the data roughly into ten groups. Record the largest values in each group as X_L and the smallest values as X_S (this is comparable to a local election). Next, record the largest X_L and the smallest X_S on the whole (comparable to a national election). $X_L = 3.68, X_S = 3.30$.

Table 2.1 Metal block thickness (in mm)

Data										X_L	X_S
3.56°	3.46	3.48	3.50	3.42ˣ	3.43	3.52	3.49	3.44	3.50	3.56	3.42
3.48	3.56°	3.50	3.52	3.47	3.48	3.46	3.50	3.56	3.38ˣ	3.56	3.38
3.41	3.37ˣ	3.47	3.49	3.45	3.44	3.50°	3.49	3.46	3.46	3.50	3.37
3.55°	3.52	3.44ˣ	3.50	3.45	3.44	3.48	3.46	3.52	3.46	3.55	3.44
3.48	3.48	3.32	3.40	3.52°	3.34	3.46	3.43	3.30ˣ	3.46	3.52	3.30ˣ
3.59	3.63°	3.59	3.47	3.38	3.52	3.45	3.48	3.31ˣ	3.46	3.63	3.31
3.40ˣ	3.54	3.46	3.51	3.48	3.50	3.68°	3.60	3.46	3.52	3.68°	3.40
3.48	3.50	3.56°	3.50	3.52	3.46ˣ	3.48	3.46	3.52	3.56	3.56	3.46
3.52	3.48	3.46	3.45	3.46	3.54°	3.54	3.48	3.49	3.41ˣ	3.54	3.41
3.41	3.45	3.34ˣ	3.44	3.47	3.47	3.41	3.48	3.54°	3.47	3.54	3.34

o: The largest value in the row $N = 100,\ X_L = 3.68$

x: The smallest value in the row $X_S = 3.30$

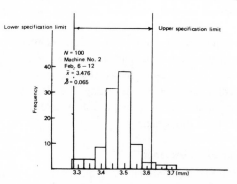

Figure 2.2 Metal block thickness

Table 2.2 Frequency table

Class no.	Class boundaries	Mid-value	Frequency tally	Frequency
1	3.275 − 3.325	3.30	///	3
2	3.325 − 3.375	3.35	///	3
3	3.375 − 3.425	3.40	̶H̶H̶ ////	9
4	3.425 − 3.475	3.45	̶H̶H̶ ̶H̶H̶ ̶H̶H̶ ̶H̶H̶ ̶H̶H̶ ̶H̶H̶ ///	33
5	3.475 − 3.525	3.50	̶H̶H̶ ̶H̶H̶ ̶H̶H̶ ̶H̶H̶ ̶H̶H̶ ̶H̶H̶ ̶H̶H̶ //	37
6	3.525 − 3.575	3.55	̶H̶H̶ ̶H̶H̶	10
7	3.575 − 3.625	3.60	///	3
8	3.625 − 3.675	3.65	/	1
9	3.675 − 3.725	3.70	/	1

$N = 100$

Table 2.3

Number of Data (N)	Number of classes (K)
Under 50	5 − 7
50 − 100	6 − 10
100 − 250	7 − 12
over 250	10 − 20

(3) The range (R) of all the data is: $R = X_L − X_S = 0.38$. This range can be divided into classes and the number of data belonging to each class can be investigated. The number of classes (the number of histogram bars) can be determined on the basis of table 2.3. However, to get the rough number of classes, take $K = 10$, and divide it into the range (R).

$$h = \frac{X_L − X_S}{K} = \frac{0.38}{10} = 0.038$$

(4) This class interval, h, which will be used as the horizontal graduation unit for the histogram, should be expressed as a multiple of an integer (the data have values of, for example, 3.56, so the units of measurement are 0.01). Here h could be considered equal to 0.04, but to make class division easier we will put it at 0.05.

(5) Class boundary, which we must determine in order to make a bar graph, is demarcated starting at one end of the range. It is troublesome when actuals fall on the class boundary. To avoid this, the boundary unit is taken as half the actual measurement unit.

9

In this case it is 0.005. In other words, the boundaries — the width of bars — will be 3.275~3.325, 3.325~3.375, etc. With check marks such as /, //, ///, ////, ////, etc, the data which belong to each class are enumerated as shown in table 2.2 and a frequency table is made. The total should correspond to N as outlined in step (1) above. (Mistakes often occur here, so be careful.)

(6) After examining the frequency table, you can get an idea of the overall picture, but if it is indicated on a graph it becomes much clearer. On graph paper, mark the class boundaries horizontally and the frequency vertically like the histogram in figure 2.2. In the blank areas write the background of the data N, average values, standard deviation, etc. If there is a company or industrial standard it is good to show this also. In this example, the specification limits on the metal blocks are 3.28~3.60 mm, so this has been recorded on the graph.

In this way, a histogram can be made. Since a histogram is a graph with bars, it is also called a bar graph. Each bar is referred to as a class. The thickness of the bar is the class interval; the numerical values corresponding to the borders of the bars are the class boundaries; the central value of the class is called representative value or mid-value. A good deal of information can be gained simply by preparing a frequency table and a histogram, as will be explained in the following section. If you wish to learn the average value $\bar{x}$ and the standard deviation s, it will be $\bar{x}$ = 3.476 and s = 0.065. (For the method of calculation, see practice problem 2.)

2.3 How to use a histogram

In this section, we will see how to read and how to use histograms.

(1) What is the shape of the distribution?

Let's try to answer the following questions by looking at the histogram in figure 2.2. What is the most common thickness of the metal blocks? How great is the dispersion? Is the distribution symmetrical? Is it skewed? Is there only one peak? Is it cliff-like? Does it look like a cogwheel? Are there any isolated bars? In other words, what are the characteristics of the product?

According to figure 2.2, most of the metal blocks are in the 3.425~3.525 thickness range. The number of blocks outside of this range that are thicker or thinner is fewer in each direction. There is a symmetrical distribution, and a 3.3 mm to 3.7 mm dispersion. There are no isolated abnormal data values.

Example 1.

One QC Circle of company A took up the problem of the reduction of scrap in the amount of metal which was trimmed from the product during manufacturing. The results of their actions are shown in figure 2.3, which is a histogram comparing the metal trimmed before and after the improvement. Not only was the amount of trimmed metal reduced (lowering of $\bar{x}$), but there was also a reduction in dispersion (lowering of s). This effect can be seen in the histogram.

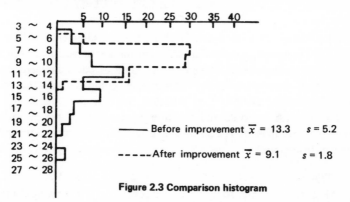

Figure 2.3 Comparison histogram

Example 2.

After measuring the parts delivered by company B, the results obtained were as shown in figure 2.4. This histogram has a cliff-like appearance on the left edge and therefore seems unusual. It is possible that before the parts were shipped from company B they were all inspected and those falling below a certain measurement value were picked out. Hereafter, it will be necessary to completely check all incoming parts and also to make certain that company B guarantees the quality of its parts, not through inspection but through improved process.

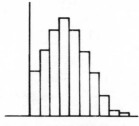

Figure 2.4 Cliff-like histogram

11

Example 3.

Data collected on the viscosity of a certain product resulted in the comb-like histogram in figure 2.5.

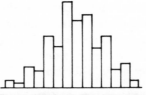

Figure 2.5 Comb-like histogram

This histogram looked abnormal, so the measurement methods were checked. It was discovered that although the instrument had been set to show only even numbers, it also gave readings of odd numbers. Thus, the amount of odd-number figures was very small compared with that of even-number figures. (Aside from mistakes such as this, be careful with histogram class intervals and the integer multiples of the measurement units, i.e. multiples of 1, 2, 3 . . . etc, otherwise you may end up with this type of histogram.)

Example 4.

All of the examples so far have been for histograms showing continuous data values. However, figures for numbers of defective parts, absentees, defects, etc (what we call discrete values) can be used as data for histograms in the same way that continuous data are. Figure 2.6. shows the number of daily machine failures in a histogram made to assist in preventive maintenance. The distribution is skewed to the right. With this kind of discrete value — number of defective parts, percentage of defective parts, number of accidents, and number of defects — the distribution of these data will often be found to assume an asymmetrical form. Of course, even with continuous data expressed in amounts, with data of 100 per cent yield and 100 per cent purity, distribution figures sometimes run on to the left because the limit is set at 100 per cent.

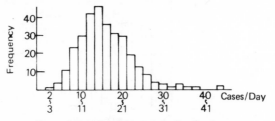

Figure 2.6 Failure occurrence distribution

(2) What is the relationship with specifications?

What is the percentage of out-of-specification products? Do products fully meet the specifications? Is the average value at the exact centre of the specification limits? Let's compare a histogram with the specifications. In figure 2.2, where the thickness of metal blocks is shown, we see that the average value is roughly in the centre of the specification limits, but the dispersion is greater than the width of the specification limits. So this dispersion must either be reduced or the specification must be re-examined.

Example 5.

A histogram showing the load characteristics of a microswitch is given in figure 2.7. There are many defective microswitches, and on the chart over half of the defects are due to load characteristics. For this reason, the data on load characteristics taken during the manufacturing process were studied by using a histogram. As can be seen clearly, the average value inclines toward the upper specification limit and the dispersion is broad. These problems were analyzed through control charts and various statistical methods; the result was a reduction in the number of defectives. This is a good example for showing how a histogram can be used to perceive the state of the manufacturing process, to help people learn what the problems are, and thus to improve process capability and reduce defects. A process capability index is used to determine whether the dispersion is sufficiently small in comparison with the specification limits.

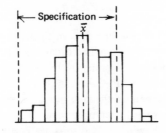

Figure 2.7 Histogram of load characteristics

(3) Is there a need to change the histogram?

When the data are stratified in accordance with the materials, machines, shifts, workers, months, etc, the distribution is probably different for each. In extreme situations, the histogram distribution may take the shape

13

of two peaks (bi-modal distribution). In the case of bi-modal distribution or broad dispersion, this distribution often includes two or more distributions which have different averages. So we must indicate this with marks (for example, *o* for materials provided by company A and *x* for materials from company B), check on the stratification factors, prepare two histograms and compare distributions. If there is no difference between these factors, the data can be drawn onto one graph.

Example 6.

A subcontracting company processed sheet metal panels for an electric machine maker, with sheet metal supplied by the parent company. However, the pressed products had many wrinkles and cracks, and they were often not the right size. Therefore, hardness tests were carried out on the sheets, and the results were shown in a histogram (figure 2.8).

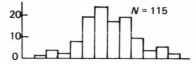

Figure 2.8 Sheet metal hardness histogram

Since the dispersion was broad, investigations were made. It was discovered that the parent company had ordered sheets from two suppliers, A and B. The sheets from these suppliers were tested separately, resulting in the stratified histograms in figure 2.9. It is clear that there is a difference in the hardness of the sheets of the two suppliers. When two separate graphs are drawn like this, such differences tend to become clear. However, it will not necessarily show up as two separate peaks in one histogram. Two separate peaks will only appear when the difference between A and B is large, a case which is quite rare. If we do not know the complete history of the data, then we cannot detect the stratification. If there is some concern that a difference may develop, then a history of the data must be kept even if it is somewhat cumbersome. This is important in improving and controlling the manufacturing process.

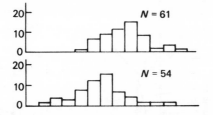

Figure 2.9 Hardness histograms by companies A and B

In addition to the histograms we have already studied, there are other relevant charts. A histogram was used to show the distribution of machine failures as in example 4, when two cases (such as 10 and 11) are classed as one. But it is also possible to count number of defectives and failures by frequency and show these in a bar graph, as in figure 2.10.

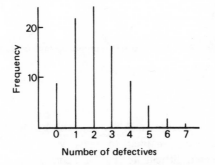

Figure 2.10 Distribution of defectives (bar graph)

This graph indicates the distribution of the number of defectives and, though there are other ways of representing this, if you know about histograms and bar graphs that should be enough. Pareto diagrams showing defectives and money lost, stratified by the pertinent reasons and conditions, can also be regarded as a kind of histogram. Figure 2.11 is a Pareto diagram that was used to focus attention on the problems which had to be overcome to reduce the number of microswitch defectives (example 5). With this chart the analysis was focused on the load characteristics (see chapter 5, Pareto diagrams).

It is convenient to make a frequency distribution table through the use of a check sheet without having to put each datum onto data sheets.

15

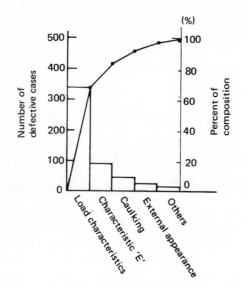

Figure 2.11 Pareto diagram of microswitch defects

Figure 2.12 shows a process capability check sheet for TV manufacturing and this table can be adapted to meet your needs. In frequency distribution it is often difficult to find time changes, so it is best to either remain constantly aware of the time while checking, or to colour-code your checks to show time differences.

If histograms are read and used as outlined, for example in monthly reports, problems will become apparent quickly and data will be much more meaningful than just mere rows of figures. Histograms are often used in charting the precision of machines or in process capability studies. Histograms can also be used effectively in our QC Circle activities when we try to eliminate defectives and improve yield and product quality, when we probe the relationship between specification and outcome, when we study abnormal data, when we examine the causes which lead to changes in the manufacturing process by stratifying the materials, equipment, etc and, finally, when we seek to upgrade the workers' awareness of quality control through actual on-the-job accomplishments.

Type	14ES	Quality characteristic	RF – SG characteristic	Specification	8 ± 2.5 db
Measuring inst.		Date	(+ 3MC)	Sample size	100
Remarks	TV		Assembly line sample control		

Class mid-value	Class Area		Representative value (x)	fx	fx²
	4.7		-9		
4.85	5.0	XX	-8	-16	108
5.15	5.3	X	-7	-7	49
5.45	5.6	XXX L.S.	-6	-18	108
5.75	5.9	X	-5	-5	25
6.05	6.2	XX	-4	-8	32
6.35	6.5	XXXXXXX	-3	-21	63
6.65	6.8	XXXXXX	-2	-12	24
6.95	7.1	XXXXXXXXXXXXXXXXXXX	-1	-19	19
7.25	7.4	XXXXXXXXXXXXXXXXX	0	0	0
7.55	7.7	XXXXXXXX	1	8	8
7.85	8.0	XXXXXXXXXXXXXXXXX	2	34	68
8.15	8.3	XXXXXX	3	18	54
8.45	8.6	XXXXXX	4	24	96
8.75	8.9	XXX	5	15	75
9.05	9.2	XX	6	12	72
9.35	9.5		7		
9.65	9.8	X	8	8	64
			9		
		Total N = 100		13	865

Class unit (h) = 0.3

Average value $\bar{x}$ =
Standard deviation s =

Code: Process quality capability

Figure 2.12 Process capability check sheet for TV manufacturing

17

Chapter 3

Cause-and-effect diagram (CE diagram)

3.1 Why does quality dispersion occur?

You have already studied how to collect data and how to make histograms, and you have seen that items produced in exactly the same way still turn out differently, as revealed in histograms. Why does this dispersion occur? In almost half of the cases, it is because of:

1) the raw materials
2) the machines or equipment
3) the work method

Raw materials differ slightly in composition according to the source of supply and there are size differences within the permitted limits. Machines may seem to be functioning in the same way, but dispersion can arise from differences in the axle sleeve fittings or because a machine is operating optimally only part of the time. In the same way work methods differ slightly although they appear to be the same.

In this way, when there is slight dispersion in raw materials, equipment and work methods, these differences can add up to a great deal of product quality dispersion in a histogram. The causal factors of dispersion are the raw material, equipment, work method, etc; these result in the dispersion of quality. This relationship is shown in figure 3.1. The relationship between cause and effect is quite clear.

The quality we want to improve and control is concretely represented by figures showing length, hardness, percentage of defectives, etc. They can be called *quality characteristics*. Chemical composition, diameters, workers, etc, which can cause the dispersion, can be called factors.

In order to illustrate on a diagram the relationship between the cause and the effect, we need to know the causes and effects in concrete forms. Therefore, the effect = quality characteristics, and cause = factors. Figure 3.1 is called a "cause-and-effect diagram". In general practice, the factors must be written in more detail to make the chart useful.

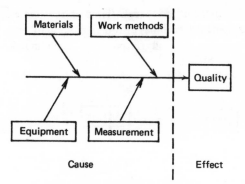

Figure 3.1 Cause-and-effect diagram

3.2 Making cause-and-effect diagrams (general steps)

The factors involved in problems with quality at our factories are almost uncountable. A cause-and-effect diagram is useful in helping us to sort out the causes of dispersion and organize the mutual relationships. We will outline the steps for making a cause-and-effect diagram. This example was drawn up on the basis of Ms Tomiko Hashimoto's article "Elimination of Volume Rotation Defects through QC Circle Activities" appearing in the magazine *Factory Work and QC* No. 33.

Step 1. Decide the quality characteristic (wobble during machine rotation). This is something we would want to improve and control. In this case we found that most of our factory defectives were due to wobble during rotating. To stop this wobble we must find its causes.

Step 2. Write the quality characteristic on the right side. Draw a broad arrow from the left side to the right side (figure 3.2)

Figure 3.2

Step 3. Write the main factors which may be causing the wobble, directing a branch arrow to the main arrow (see figure 3.3). It is recommended to group the major possible causal factors

19

of dispersion into such items as raw materials (materials), equipment (machines or tools), method of work (workers) and measuring method (inspection). Each individual group will form a branch.

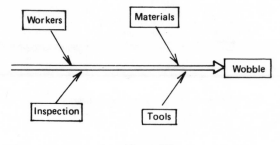

Figure 3.3

Step 4. Now, onto each of these branch items, write in the detailed factors which may be regarded as the causes. These will be like twigs. And onto each of these, write in even more detailed factors, making smaller twigs (figure 3.4). If you keep the following in mind, you cannot help but find the cause of the problem.

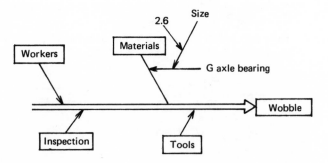

Figure 3.4

1) Why do production process defects occur? Because of machine wobble (dispersion). Therefore machine wobble is a quality characteristic.

2) Why does the machine wobble (dispersion) occur? Because of dispersion in the materials. 'Materials' is written on the diagram as a branch.

3) Why does dispersion in the materials occur? Because of the dispersion in the G axle bearing. The G axle bearing becomes a twig on the branch.

4) Why does dispersion in the G axle bearing occur? Because of the dispersion in the size of the G axle bearing. Size becomes a twig on the twig.

5) Why does dispersion in the size of the G axle bearing occur? Because of the dispersion at the 2.6 mm point. The 2.6 mm point thus becomes a twig on the twig on the twig.

In this way we add to a cause-and-effect diagram until it fully shows the causes of the dispersion. Figure 3.5 gives the completed form.

Note: Your members must speak frankly with one another (brainstorming method) to build up a cause-and-effect diagram.

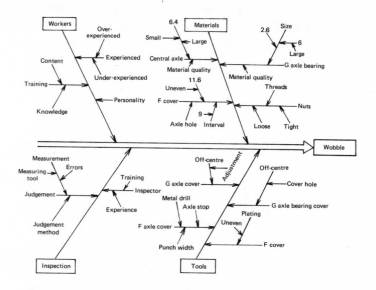

Figure 3.5 Cause-and-effect diagram for wobbling (dispersion analysis)

Step 5. Finally, one must check to make certain that all the items that may be causing dispersion are included in the diagram. If they are, and the relationships of causes to effects are properly illustrated, then the diagram is complete.

3.3 Various methods for making cause-and-effect diagrams

The possible causes of dispersion in the quality characteristics are arranged in the cause-and-effect diagrams in such a way that all the relationships are clearly noticeable. There are various methods for making cause-and-effect diagrams depending on how you organize and arrange them. These methods can be divided into the three following types:

1) Dispersion analysis type
2) Production process classification type
3) Cause enumeration type

(1) Dispersion analysis type

The cause-and-effect diagram we just studied falls under this type. The secret of making it is to keep asking: "Why does this dispersion occur?" Remember to bear in mind that each and every dispersion can be rectified. The strong point of this type is that, since it involves the breaking of dispersions, it helps organize and relate the factors for dispersion. Its weak point is that the form the diagram takes often depends on the person making it, and that sometimes small causes are not picked up.

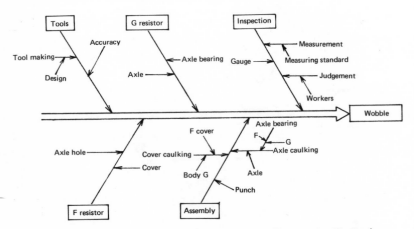

Figure 3.6 Cause-and-effect diagram for wobbling (process classification)

22

(2) Production process classification type

With this method, the diagram's main line follows the production process and all things that may affect the quality are added to the process stage. If the cause-and-effect diagram shown in figure 3.5 were drawn as a production process classification type diagram, it would appear as in figure 3.6. This type can also be done as an assembly line diagram with the causes added. Figure 3.7 is an example of this, showing how scarring occurs during steel tubing. Remember that dispersion occurs during the production process, so go through the steps in the manufacturing process one by one to seek the causes. The strong point of this type is that, since it

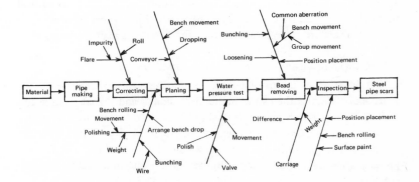

Figure 3.7 Cause-and-effect diagram for steel pipe scars (process classification)

follows the sequence of the production process, it is easy to make and understand. Its weak point is that similar causes appear again and again, and causes due to a combination of more than one factor are difficult to illustrate.

(3) Cause enumeration type

In this type all the possible causes are simply listed. When doing this, everyone's ideas are necessary and the use of a blackboard is helpful when listing the causes. These causes must be organized in accordance with the product quality showing the relationship between the cause and the effect, and then a cause-and-effect diagram can be made. The completed diagrams might resemble figure 3.5, but in the beginning, simply list as many of the possible causes as you can think of. Remember not to confine your thoughts to types of cause or process order but to think as freely as you

23

can. The real cause or the hint for a cure will come out of this kind of free thought. The advantage of this type is that all causes are listed and thus no major causes are missed. Also, by considering the relationship between the cause and the effect, the diagram is quite complete. Its disadvantage is that it is difficult to relate the twig causes to the result, and thus the diagram is difficult to draw.

3.4 How to use a cause-and-effect diagram

Cause-and-effect diagrams are drawn to clearly illustrate the various causes affecting product quality by sorting out and relating the causes. Therefore a good cause-and-effect diagram is one that fits the purpose, and there is no one definite form. The important thing is that it meets each purpose. There are several ways of using them, but the main ones are:

(1) Making a cause-and-effect diagram is educational in itself

Get ideas from as many people as possible when making one. Ask everyone: "What is the cause of the dispersion?" and "What relationship and effect does that have on the quality?" These consultations with others mean presenting one's experience and techniques. Everyone taking part in making this diagram will gain new knowledge. Even people who do not yet know a great deal about their jobs can learn a lot from making a cause-and-effect diagram or merely studying a completed one.

(2) A cause-and-effect diagram is a guide for discussion

A discussion cannot be purposeful when the speakers stray from their topic. When a cause-and-effect diagram serves as a focus for the discussion, everyone knows the topic and how far the discussion has advanced. Straying from the topic and repetitions of complaints and grievances are avoided. The conclusion on what action to take is reached faster. In view of this, a cause-and-effect diagram can be said to be the guide in carrying out discussions.

(3) The causes are sought actively and the results are written in on the diagram

Whenever an unusual quality characteristic is discovered, actively seek the factor behind it. This is one of the fundamentals of QC. If you find the real factor, repeat the steps you took to find the cause on the cause-and-effect diagram.

If you get lost in the diagram searching for the factor or you can't tie the real factor down, this shows that the diagram causes are not the real causes of the dispersion — so reconstruct your diagram in accordance with the actual steps you took. If the true factor is not written on the diagram, be sure you write it in.

(4) Data are collected with a cause-and-effect diagram

When a change occurs in quality, it is important to find the defect percentage, dispersion range, etc. But these figures only show what has happened; they do not provide any solution. In cases of quality changes, seek the causes thoroughly and once you have found the true causes, check and record them in the cause-and-effect diagram as in figure 3.8. Here it shows that on March 15 the 6.4 mm section of the central axle was actually smaller than the specified size and caused the wobble. In this way we can detect the true cause which can lead us to action. This simple procedure of making circles enables the data to be highly reliable (high quality) and effective in actual factory works.

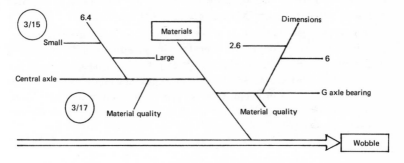

Figure 3.8

(5) A cause-and-effect diagram shows the level of technology

If a cause-and-effect diagram can be drawn up thoroughly, it means those doing it know quite a bit about the production process. In other words, the higher the level of technology of the workers, the better the cause-and-effect diagram turns out to be.

If you use the following marks on your cause-and-effect diagrams you can understand the level of ability in your factory.

a. When the relationship between the quality characteristics and a cause can be shown quantitatively in exact figures, put a box around it. In the case of the wobble, a 5 micron difference caused a 2 per cent wobble.

$$\boxed{\text{off-centre}}$$

b. When the relationships between the quality characteristic and cause are difficult to show in figures but it is still definite that relationships exist, the causal factor should be underlined.

<u>tightening of nuts</u>

c. When there is no real proof that a certain cause is really related to the problem, do not mark it in any way. There will thus be few causes in boxes or underlined. The more causes that can be put in boxes or underlined, the higher the technological level of the workers concerned.

(6) A cause-and-effect diagram can be used for any problem

We have discussed the cause-and-effect diagram in relation to quality. But since this kind of diagram illustrates the relationship between the cause and the effect in a rational manner, it can be used in any situation. The cause-and-effect diagram shown in figure 3.9 was made to improve mutual relations between QC Circles in different companies. In this way, a cause-and-effect diagram can be made not only for quality matters but for quantity, material amounts and even for safety, work attendance, or any kind of personnel problem. Our aim is to get results; since measures are to be taken against the cause, if we do not know the relationship between cause and effect of a problem, then we cannot take any action to solve it. A cause-and-effect diagram shows us most clearly the causes so we can take action quickly.

(7) Bad cause-and-effect diagrams

A cause generally consists of many complex elements. Therefore, cause-and-effect diagrams usually turn out to be rather complicated, like the one in figure 3.10. If one turns out looking like the one in figure 3.11, it means that your knowledge of the manufacturing process is still too shallow. Also, if your diagram only lists five or six causes, even though the form is correct, it cannot be considered a good diagram.

3.5 The development of cause-and-effect diagrams and the future

The first cause-and-effect diagram was developed by Professor Kaoru Ishikawa of the University of Tokyo in the summer of 1953, while he was

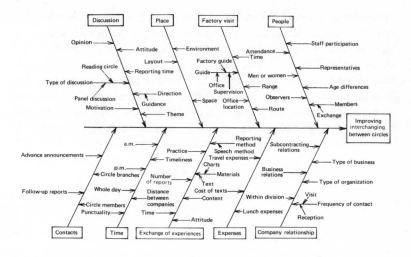

Figure 3.9

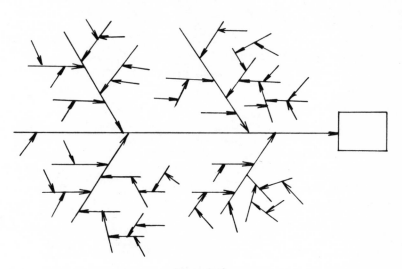

Figure 3.10

27

explaining to some engineers at a factory of the Kawasaki Steel Works the fact that various factors can be sorted out and related in such and such a way. In this sense, the cause-and-effect diagram is a QC method that originated in Japan. It later came into wide use throughout Japanese industry and became indispensible for carrying out quality control. The diagram spread to other countries; it is sometimes called an Ishikawa diagram. As mentioned previously, the cause-and-effect diagram is used not only for QC problems — it can be applied to the solution of any problem. It is a guide to concrete action. The more use that is made of it the more effective it becomes. And effective use of cause-and-effect diagrams is a prime step for promoting QC activities.

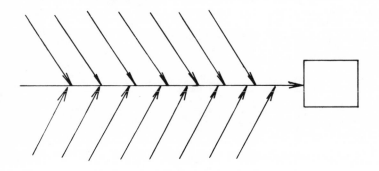

Figure 3.11

Chapter 4

Check sheets

4.1 Quality control and check sheets

We can very well say that the basis of statistical quality control is the full utilization of each technique and of the data resulting from these techniques. Indeed, the word 'statistical' implies data. Data reflect facts. Where control depends on data, those data must be correct. No matter how carefully incorrect data are analyzed, the results will be meaningless. Data must be collected carefully and accurately. Also, the purpose for which the data are being collected must be quite clear. If one is not careful, it is easy to forget the purpose for which the data are collected. Furthermore, it often happens that the data collected to control the production process, to make the relationship between a cause and effect clear, to determine the strength of materials, etc, are not being used for the intended purpose. Sometimes, no action is taken in spite of the definite cause and effect.

Data without a clear purpose or unreliable data are worth nothing. The essential with data is that the purpose be clear and the data reflect the truth. Then the next problem is to make the data easy to obtain and to use. This is why many check sheets are used in factories. Check sheets have many purposes, but the main one is to make it easy to compile the data and in such a form that they may be used easily, and analyzed automatically. In this chapter, we shall study the various check sheets.

4.2 Function of check sheets

Factory check sheets have the following functions:

1. Production process distribution checks
2. Defective item checks
3. Defect location checks
4. Defective cause checks
5. Check-up confirmation checks
6. Others

4.3 Check sheet for production process distribution

The size, weight and diameter of parts are known as continuous data. In a process where these data are obtained, the distribution that they show comes into question. A histogram can be used in investigating the distribution of the process characteristics and, with this as the base, the average value and the dispersion can be computed and the manner of dispersion studied. However, when preparing a histogram, to collect a great deal of data first, and then make a frequency distribution table from these data, is an unnecessary double task. When investigating the distribution of

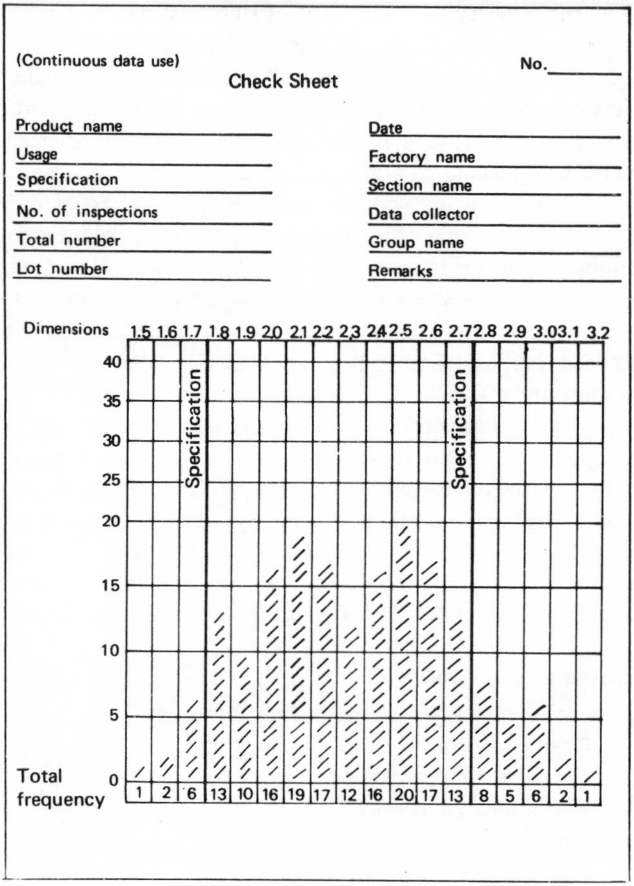

Figure 4.1 Check sheet for production process distribution

a production process, individual data are not of major importance; it is usually sufficient to ascertain the form of the distribution and relationships to the specification limits. It is therefore simpler to sort the data as they are collected. Figure 4.1 is an example of a frequency distribution form in which the figures have already been indicated, and all the data collector has to do is to make check marks. In this way the frequency distribution can already be ascertained once the data have been collected. This is much faster and simpler than recording each value separately and then making the table.

However, changes in value over a period of time do not reveal themselves in this form. Therefore, when using this form, it is necessary to be certain at the stage of making checks that there are no time lags in the data. Also, the person collecting the data must be careful not to forget to make any check marks, as mischecks are almost impossible to discover later. When the machines, materials, or workers differ — that is, when the conditions influencing the data differ — it is best to use a separate check sheet each time and to compare them later. When using a single check sheet, for different data sources, you can also use different colours in making your marks, or use different types of marks. When the check sheet is completed, examine it for the following two things:

(1) Does the distribution assume the shape of a bell, i.e. single-peaked and neat, or are there two peaks? Are the values skewed to one side and are there any isolated values?

(2) Check the relationship existing between the actual distribution and the specification limits. Is the centre of the distribution close to that of the specification limits? Is the width of the distribution greater than that of the specifications? Find out the actual percentage that is outside of the specification limit and the measures to be taken to reduce these defectives.

If the shape of the distribution is not good then the reason must be found and corrected.

4.4 Defective item checks

In order to reduce the number of defectives it is necessary to know the kind of defects and their percentages. Since every defect has different causes, it is of no use just to list the total number of defects. We must find the number of defects caused by each reason and appropriate action must be taken, beginning with places where there are many defects. Figure 4.2 is an example of the check sheet used in a resin production plant. Whenever a worker on the pressing line came up with a defect, a mark was

31

made in the appropriate column. Thus, at the end of a day's work, one could immediately see the number of defects and on which item they occurred.

The percentages for each reason should not come out the same; they will be larger for some and smaller for others. By using a check sheet such as the one in figure 4.2, you will obtain data that should enable you to make corrections in the production process where necessary.

However, this check sheet, like the check sheet in figure 4.1, will not show changes in values over a time period. For example, some defects may be produced mainly in the morning, or there may be a tendency for the first defect to cause further defects of the same kind. This tendency with time cannot be read from the completed sheet. As this sort of information is extremely important in improving the production process, the person making the check sheet should have a knowledge of statistical methods. It must be decided in advance what kind of check will be made if two or more kinds of defects are found in one product, or if a defect derives from two or more causes; the person doing the checking must be thorough. It is also important to examine several sheets in the chronological order of completion to determine trends of defect occurrence. If the occurrence of

---

Check Sheet

Product:	Date:
Manufacturing stage: final insp.	Factory:
	Section:
Type of defect: scar, incomplete, misshapen	Inspector's name:
	Lot no.:
Total no. inspected: 2530	Order no.:

Remarks: all items inspected

Type	Check	Sub-total
Surface scars	HH HH HH HH HH HH //	32
Cracks	HH HH HH HH ///	23
Incomplete	HH HH HH HH HH HH HH HH ///	48
Misshapen	////	4
Others	HH ///	8
	Grand total:	115
Total rejects	HH HH HH HH HH HH HH HH HH HH HH HH HH HH HH HH HH /	86

Figure 4.2 Defective item check sheet

32

the major defect suddenly declines, you know that your actions were successful. If defects in general decline, it means that your control has improved in general. If the major defect is different each month but the overall fraction defective does not fall, it means that your control is not fully adequate.

4.5 Defect location check sheet

With most products there are various defects that are connected with the external appearance, such as scars and dirt. At many factories efforts are being made to reduce these kinds of defects. In eliminating this sort of problem, the defect location check sheet is extremely useful. Usually, this kind of check sheet is meant to be placed in the sketch or drawing of the product so that the location of the defects can be investigated. Figure 4.3 is a check sheet used to examine bubbles in laminated automobile windshield glass. The location and form of bubbles was indicated on the check sheet, and it was found that most of the bubbles were on the right side. Upon investigation it was discovered that the pressure used in laminating was out of balance — the right side receiving less pressure. The machine was adjusted and the formation of bubbles was eliminated almost completely.

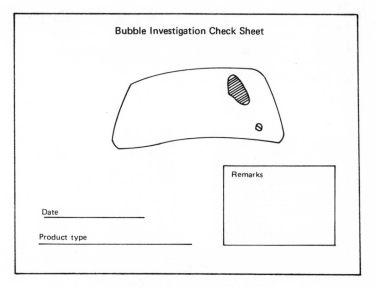

Figure 4.3 Defect location check sheet

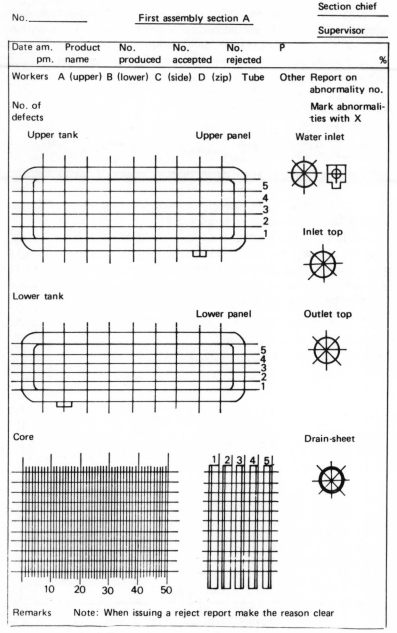

Figure 4.4 Radiator leak check sheet

Figure 4.4 is a check sheet for recording water leakage in radiators. Most leaks were found at the tank connections and, after correcting the solder composition in the assembly line, the occurrence of leaks dropped by 50 per cent.

As can be seen from the examples above, this type of check sheet leads to quick action and is an important tool for process analysis. Note the part where the defect occurs, and consider why it is concentrated on this part. If you carefully examine the process with this in mind, you will discover the cause. When using this kind of check sheet, sketch the parts of the product and draw in partitions to make it easy to stratify defects. The partition lines should be drawn in evenly (at even intervals).

4.6 Defective cause check sheet

The check sheets already mentioned are used for investigating certain aspects of defects, such as the location. For a further investigation of the cause, another check sheet is sometimes used. Generally, to investigate defective causes, data concerning causes and corresponding data on effects (percentage defectives, yield, etc) are arranged so the relationship between cause and effect is clear. These are later analyzed through the use of the stratification by cause factors or through the use of scatter diagrams. In simple cases, corresponding data can be used directly from the check sheet.

Equipment	Worker	Monday am	Monday pm	Tuesday am	Tuesday pm	Wednesday am	Wednesday p m	Thursday a m	Thursday p m	Friday a m	Friday p m	Saturday a m	Saturday p m
Machine 1	A	00X●	0X	000	0XX	000X XX●	0000 XXX	0000 X●●	0XX	0000	00	0	XX●
	B	0XX●	000X X0	0000 00XX	000X X	0000 00XX ●	0000 00X●	0000 0X	000X ●●	00XX ●	0000 0	00X	000● X0X
Machine 2	C	00X	0X	00	●	0000 0	0000 00X	00	0●	00△	00□	△0	0□
	D	00X	0X	00	000●	000● △	0000 0X	0●0	00△	00△△ □	0 ●●	□00X	XX0

Figure 4.5 Defective cause check sheet

35

Figure 4.5 is an example of this type of check sheet. It is used to record defectives in bakelite knobs, and the occurrence of defectives is illustrated separately by each category: by workers, by machines, by dates and by types of defects. The symbols are:

O : surface scratch
X : blowhole
△ : defective finishing
● : improper shape
□ : others

With just a glance, you can see that worker B produced the most defectives. Also, on Wednesday all workers had numerous defectives. Upon investigation, it was found that worker B was not changing his metal machine parts well and that the materials used on Wednesday were faulty in composition, thus creating a greater tendency to produce defectives.

This type of check sheet attempts to link cause and effect, so it sometimes becomes a bit complex. In place of this, but for the same purpose, you can prepare a check sheet using a cause-and-effect diagram. In other words, draw a cause-and-effect diagram for easy use at the factory and, when the situation of the defect and the reason for it is found, make a mark at the appropriate arrow. This will give you some guide as to which cause you should concentrate on.

4.7 Check-up confirmation check sheet

The purpose of this check sheet is different from that of the other check sheets we have studied, which were concerned mainly with quality characteristics such as defectives and defects. Figure 4.6 shows the check sheet used in an automobile assembly plant.

This check sheet is used in the final phase of assembly, the "tester line", which is for checking and finishing all the work that has already been done throughout the complex automobile manufacturing process. The purpose of this phase is not assembly itself but to carry out a comprehensive check-up of the quality that has been built up through the previous process phases. As you can see from figure 4.6, there are over 100 check items; this check sheet is used to make certain that all the tests are made without fail. With checks as complicated and long as this one there is a tendency to test the same thing twice or to forget to make important tests in the given time. In order to carry out all checks thoroughly and without fail, all the tests are listed beforehand on the check sheet and a mark must be made for each item as you proceed with the check-up. This way

Test Line Check Sheet		Date: Inspector:		Shift:		

Alignment
1. Toe-in   OK
2. Turning inside right   OK   left   OK
3. Tracking tyre allowance
4. Headlight adjustment   Focus R/L   Switching R/L

Brakes

1.	Foot brake	Front	OK	Smooth	NG	Difference	NG
		Rear	OK	"	NG	"	NG
2.	Hand brake		OK	"	NG	"	NG

Remarks

_____

_____

Starting

1.	Brake oil level	6.	Ignition pilot light
2.	Oil gauge action	7.	Temp. gauge action
3.	Choke action	8.	Idle adjustment
4.	Fan belt tension	9.	E button
5.	Starter action	10.	Resistance glow plug

Lamp switch

1.	Headlights R/L	8.	Stop lights R/L
2.	Headlight pilot light	9.	Light switch
3.	Dimmer switch R/L	10.	Direction indicators R/L
4.	Panel lights	11.	Emergency lights R/L
5.	Parking lights R/L	12.	Turn pilot light
6.	Tail lights R/L	13.	Overhead light
7.	Licence plate light	14.	Wiper SW

Horn

1.	Sound	2.	Button action

Accelerator, brake, clutch

1.	Pedal play A/B/C	5.	Hand brake return
2.	Pedal pressure A/B/C	6.	Pedal spongy A/B/C
3.	Pedal return A/B/C	7.	Pedal clearance
4.	No. of notches visible on hand brake lever		

Running test

1.	Vibration at low to medium speeds	13.	Gear wt. 1-2-3-4 R
2.	Ignition timing	14.	Gear shifting 1-2-3-4 R
3.	Noise	15.	Gear grinding 1-2-3-4 R.N.
4.	Stalling	16.	Companion flange sound
5.	Accelerating	17.	Clutch sound
6.	W pump sound	18.	Diff sound stall accele- ration
7.	F pump sound	19.	SP meter action
8.	Alternator sound	20.	Tyre wobble ft. R/L r. R/L
9.	Clutch action	21.	Brake grab R/L
10.	Lever position	22.	Exhaust leaks; manifold; muffler
11.	Selector weight		
12.	Lever return		

Steering wheel

1.	Stiffness	5.	Catching
2.	Play	6.	Handle drop R/L
3.	Return	7.	Jack
4.	Grinding		

Rasping sounds

_____

Figure. 4.6 Automobile test line check sheet

Oil; gas; water leaks		

(1: none; 2: smudge; 3: puddle; 4: drip; 5: flow)

1.	E oil pan bolt ( )	4.	E pressure SW ( )
2.	E oil pan drain ( )	5.	E timing cover ( )
3.	E rear plate ( )	6.	E oil filter ( )
7.	M case cover ( )	9.	M drain plug ( )
8.	M ext oil seal ( )	10.	M freezer ( )
11.	St housing cover ( )		
12.	D gear carrier facing ( )	14.	D breather ( )
13.	D drain plug ( )	15.	D companion ( )
16.	B master cylinder ( )		
17.	B 3-way conn. front and back ( )		
18.	B oil cylinder front R/L ( ) rear R/L ( )		
19.	B hose front R/L ( ) rear R/L ( )		
20.	Gas tank ( )	21.	Gas pipe conn. ( )
22.	W rachet upper/lower ( )	25.	W hose upper/lower ( )
23.	W drain ( )	26.	W cylinder block ( )
24.	W pump ( )		

Parts fastenings

1. F axle F pin fastened R/L
2. F axle shock pin fastened R/L
3. F axle U-bolt fastened R/L
4. R axle F-pin fastened R/L
5. R axle shock pin fastened R/L
6. R axle U-bolt fastened R/L
7. R shock absorb. fastened R/L
8. P shaft fastened
9. Wheel nut fastened front back R/L

10. St. housing fastened
11. Tie rod fastened R/L
12. Remote control lock nut fastened

13. F brake hose fastened R/L
14. Brake tube fastened
15. R brake hose fastened
16. Fuel pipe clamp
17. Undercoat clearance

18.
19.
20.
21.
22.
23.
24.
25.

Sideslip	First test OK NG ( )
	Second test OK

Windshield washer	
	1. OK NG
	2. Wiper motion
	3. Wiper noise pressure speed clearance

Figure. 4.6 Automobile test line check sheet

there is no danger of forgetting, and the check sheet remains as a permanent record that can be referred back to later if necessary. When many and varied jobs have to be done in the same step, this type of check will be useful to avoid mistakes.

Figure 4.7 is an equipment maintenance check sheet. Frequent checks must be made to keep equipment working efficiently and trouble-free. Some checks or tests are made daily, others weekly, still others monthly, or at fixed intervals. With even the slightest absent-mindedness, it is easy to forget a check-up or even whether a test was really made or not. In such cases a check sheet helps you carry out your work with certainty; it will also clarify forgotten test items.

Sewage Tank Maintenance Check — Equipment section

Area	Place	Motor size Manuf. No.	Are checked	No.	Check date / Contents of inspection	Weather	Temp.	Checker's name	Chief	Clerk / Check	Worker / Check	Group chief / Remarks
Electric Panel			No fuse breaker Iron box opener and closer	1	Condition of opening and closing?							
				2	Is panel warm?							
				3	Blade and blade receiver content?							
				4	Proper fuse?							
				5	Any handle obstructions?							
			Selector switch	1	Is knob showing?							
				2	Condition under motion test?							
			Snap switch	3	Is locking nut loose?							
				4	Contact points in contact?							
			Gauges	1	Condition of current flow?							
				2	How many amps?						A	
				3	How many volts?						V	
				4	Pilot lamp broken or burned out?							
			Front-less switch	1	Does buzzer ring?							
				2	Does front-less switch move?							
			Buzzer	3	Any unusual noise or smell?							
			3E relay	4	Does 3E relay operate?		60%			Sec.		
				5	"		80%			Sec.		
			Magnet switch	6	"		100%			Sec.		
				7	Is magnet jumping?							
				8	Contact points in contact?							

Figure 4.7 Equipment maintenance check sheet

40

With this type of check sheet, the checks listed should be in the same order that they are actually made.

4.8 Other check sheets

Of course there are many other kinds of check sheets that are used in factories. Figure 4.8 shows a work sampling check sheet. Work sampling is a method for analyzing working time. The total work is divided into main work, preparatory work, allowance time, etc. Then, the percentage devoted to each is examined by an intensive repetition of observing the work contents momentarily at randomly selected times. In other words, the number of workers engaged in main work, preparatory work, or who have spare time is checked at certain times and the percentages are found as the result of repeating these checks. The check sheet in figure 4.8 is used for this sort of checking.

Work Sampling Check Sheet

Checker:_____ Object of check _____ Date _____
Method:_____ Weather_____

Item	Checks	Total	%
Processing	HH HH // ————	463	65%
Planning	HH HH // ————	157	22%
Transport	HH // ———————	32	8%
Break-down	HH HH /	11	4%
Others	HH //	7	1%
Total		670	100%

Figure 4.8 Work sampling check sheet

Various kinds of check sheets have been dealt with here. But always remember the purpose for collecting data and then try to make the most appropriate and simplest check sheet that will meet your needs adequately. I believe many data are already being collected in your factory. However, it is worthwhile to reconsider the purpose of the exercise and make studies to see whether any points can be improved for easier and more efficient collection of data.

Chapter 5

Pareto diagrams

5.1 What is a Pareto diagram?

There are many aspects of factory production that must be improved: defectives, time allocation, cost savings, etc. In fact, each problem consists of so many smaller problems that it is difficult to know just how to go about solving them. And a definite basis is needed for any action.

Table 5.1 Record of defectives

Date:	Number inspected:	$N = 2165$	
Defective items	Number of defectives	Per cent defective	Per cent defective of total defectives
Caulking	198	9.1%	47.6
Fitting	25	1.2%	6.0
Connecting	103	4.8%	24.8
Torque	18	0.8%	4.3
Gapping	72	3.3%	17.3
Total	416	19.2%	100

Table 5.1 gives data on defectives from a certain process. Although in the process the defectives are lumped together as coming from "inadequate operations", they can be divided into the following five headings: caulking, fitting, connection, improper torque, and gapping. These defective categories broken down by their nature are called defective items. Data from this table have been made into a bar graph (figure 5.1).

In Fig. 5.1., the left vertical axis shows the number of defectives for each defective item and the right vertical axis shows the percent of composition for each defective item over the total defectives. The horizontal axis lists the defective items starting with the most frequent one on the left to the least frequent on the extreme right, the rest being arranged by order of magnitude. Cumulative total of the number of

(pieces)

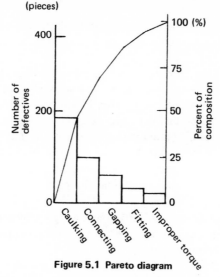

Figure 5.1 Pareto diagram

defectives for each defective item is shown by the line graph. This type of graph is called a Pareto Diagram.

A Pareto diagram, such as this, indicates which problem we should solve first in eliminating defects and improving the operation. According to this graph, we should tackle caulking first because it forms the tallest bar. The next most significant defective item is the second tallest bar, connecting. Although this may all appear very simple, bar graphs are extremely useful in factory quality control. I will simply mention here that it is much easier to see which defects are most important with a bar graph than by using a table of numbers only. The advantages of this graph will be explained in the third section of this chapter.

5.2 How to make a Pareto diagram

Anyone who has ever made a bar graph can easily make a Pareto diagram. Although some of you may already have had experience in drawing bar graphs, please read the following as a review of sorts.

Step 1. Make certain of the classifications items you will use in the graph. For example, graphs could list items according to kinds of defectives, defects, work groups, products, size, damage, etc. (If your data records are not classified or itemized you cannot construct a Pareto diagram. Revise your check sheet so that your data will be itemized.)

43

Step 2. Decide on the period of time to be illustrated on your graph. In other words, from what time to what time it will cover. There is no prescribed period of time, so naturally the period will vary according to the situation. It is preferable that the period be set conveniently such as one week, two weeks (half a month), one month, three months (quarterly) etc, but for some situations it could also be one day, two days or four hours. The important thing to bear in mind is to try to keep the period for all related graphs the same so that you can compare them later.

Step 3. Total the frequency of occurrence for each item for the period you decided upon. The total for each item will be shown by the length of the bar.

Step 4. Draw horizontal and vertical axes on graph paper and demarcate the vertical axis in the proper units (such as number of defectives). To make the graph easy to read, try to mark it off so one scale unit is 0.1, 0.2, 0.5 or 1, etc and your numbers are on the lines of the graph paper. In setting the position of 0 or 10's, you should make use of the bold line on the graph paper drawn in at regular intervals of tens (e.g. on a graph paper with 1 mm blocks, the bold lines will be drawn in every 10 mm). Do not write in every number on the vertical line. Use alternate squares on the paper for values such as 2, 4, 6 . . . , or skip squares and write in only 0, 5, 10, etc. At the top or the side of the vertical axis write in the explanation of the units.

Step 5. Under the horizontal axis, write in the most important item first, then the next most important, and so on, so the most frequent defective item is shown on the far left. When there are many items with little frequency, however, they can be categorized together as 'others' and shown on the extreme right. (See Fig. 5.7)

Step 6. Draw in the bars. The height of the bar will correspond to the value on the vertical axis. Keep the width of the bars the same and each bar should be in contact with its neighbour as the area of the bar represents the no. of defectives.

Step 7. Plot a line graph of the cumulative total for each item.

Step 8. Title the graph and write briefly the source of the data on which the graph is based. If there is no title, or if no one can tell when the data were taken, under what conditions (the inspection method, inspector, whether before or after modification, etc), the number of inspected parts, the total number of defects and defectives, then of course, it is of no use whatsoever. With quality control, the source of the data must be clear.

5.3 How to use a Pareto diagram

(1) A Pareto diagram is the first step in making improvements

In making improvements, the following things are important:

1) that everyone concerned cooperate;

2) that it has a strong impact;

3) that a concrete goal be selected.

If all the workers try to make improvements individually and there is no definite basis for their efforts, then a lot of energy will produce few results.

A Pareto diagram is very useful in obtaining the cooperation of all concerned because one look at it tells everyone what the major problem

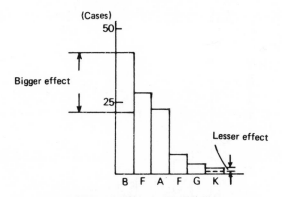

Figure 5.2 Effort for and effect of improvement

is — it is the two or three taller bars which account for the majority of the problems, the smaller bars being lesser causes.

Experience has shown us that it is easier to reduce a tall bar by half than to reduce a short bar to zero. If we can reduce the tallest bar in figure 5.2 — the one which accounts for the most defectives — it will have been a considerable accomplishment. If it requires the same effort to reduce the tall bar by half as to reduce a short bar by half, there is no doubt about which should be selected as the target. To reduce the minor defectives — represented by the short bars — by half or to zero, would require tremendous efforts since there are more or less inevitable defectives occurring now and then.

Because we have to produce results with limited capacities, manpower and time, we must cooperate to achieve improvements by concentrating on the worthy targets, that is, the item or items represented by the tallest and taller bars on the Pareto diagram. The value of Pareto diagrams is that they teach us which factors are most important and therefore deserve our concentrated attention. As you have already understood, the Pareto diagram is an indispensible instrument for knowing exactly the target to choose on which efforts for improvement should be concentrated. Thus, we can say that a Pareto diagram is the first step to making improvements.

(2) Pareto diagrams can be applied for improvement in all aspects

As has been mentioned, improvement in the factory is not only a question of improvement of quality — there are also the problem of

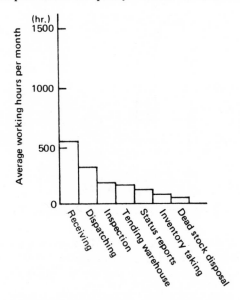

Figure 5.3 Pareto diagram of cumulative hours spent by warehouse workers on different jobs

efficiency, conservation of materials and energy saving costs, safety, and others. Whatever the problem, if the question is improvement, Pareto diagrams can be drawn up and applied. And, as explained previously, Pareto diagrams are the first step.

The diagram shown in figure 5.3 was used to improve the efficiency of office work. The horizontal axis shows the various jobs of workers in a warehouse. The vertical axis shows the number of hours spent on each job. On the basis of this graph, the goal for improvement was receival, and good results were obtained.

Figure 5.4 shows a diagram that was used to improve machine breakdown prevention and preventive maintenance planning. The horizontal axis shows the location of trouble spots. On the basis of this graph, the goal for improvement was the oil pressure line, and a cause-and-effect diagram was made. Improvement was carried out and the results were very good.

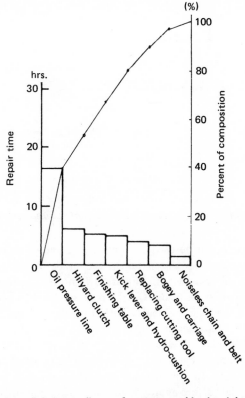

Figure 5.4 Pareto diagram for cutter machine breakdowns

Figures 5.5 and 5.6 are Pareto diagrams that were used to improve safety. Figure 5.5 shows the number of accidents by injured part of the body. Further, it shows that the most frequent injuries involved fingers. However, this information alone was not enough, so figure 5.6, showing the causes of finger injuries, was prepared. From this diagram it can be seen that the chief cause of injuries was fingers being struck: consequently, appropriate measures were taken.

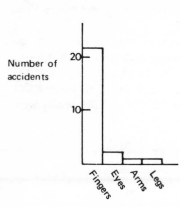

Figure 5.5 Injury Pareto diagram

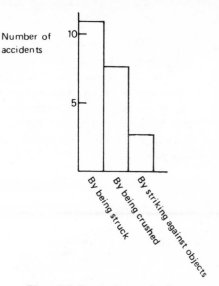

Figure 5.6 Pareto diagram for finger injury accident causes

(3) Pareto diagrams show whether your attempts at improvement produce results

Pareto diagrams can be used to confirm the impact of improvement. If effective measures have been taken, the order of the items on the horizontal axis will usually shift. Figure 5.7 shows diagrams before and after improvements were made. On the basis of the before-improvement diagram on the left, the problem of defectives due to improper rotation was selected for improvement. The items for inspection in the major process were determined to eliminate the possible factors causing improper rotation. The workers engaged in these tasks were asked to check the results of their work. In this way, the diagram on the right was obtained.

Comparing the before-improvement and after-improvement graphs it can be seen that improper rotation dropped to the second most important source of trouble, the first place being taken by the previous second source, noise.

Note 1

If the percent of composition of Fig. 5.7 is plotted on the left vertical axis as in Fig. 5.8, the bar representing noise in the after-improvement graph becomes taller than the one in the before-improvement graph

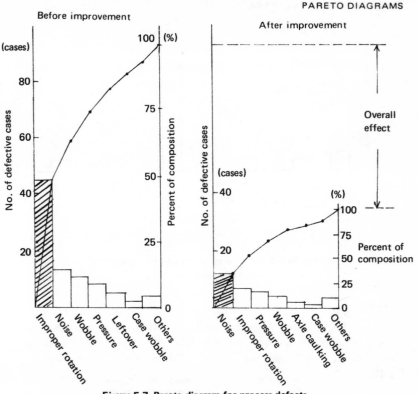

Figure 5.7 Pareto diagram for process defects

as if the defectives due to noise were increased. In a series of Pareto diagrams drawn with the same intervals, the length of the bar for each item may change. But the reason the defectives due to noise seem to be increased in the after-improvement graph is mainly because the defectives due to rotation declined sharply after the improvement. As a consequence, the total number of defectives also fell, causing the percentage of defectives due to noise to increase. As one can easily get confused in this way, it is better not to plot the percent of composition on the left vertical axis. By making graphs as Fig. 5.7, this kind of confusion can be avoided and the decrease in the total number of defectives will clearly be recognized.

Note 2

Generally, if improvement measures are taken, and proven effective, the order of the bars will change. But if daily control (control for maintenance) is carried out thoroughly, the bar order will not change and the height of the longer bars will gradually fall.

49

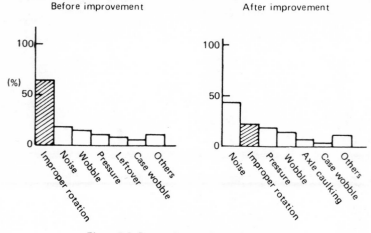

Figure 5.8 Pareto diagram for process defects
— bad example —

Note 3

If a series of Pareto diagrams made at certain time intervals show marked changes in order, although there has been no attempt at improvement, it indicates that control of daily work in that process is insufficient.

5.4 Try to have the vertical axis represent amounts of money

All the Pareto diagrams we have studied so far have had the vertical axis represent case numbers or time or precentages of cases. If case numbers and percentages are proportional to monetary amounts, this is acceptable. But in many cases, the amount of monetary loss per defective or defect varies from situation to situation. In such cases, try to express the vertical axis in monetary units which would correspond to the number of defects or defectives. This way the graph is that much more useful. In order to learn the approximate amount of money lost which would correspond to each defective or defect, it may be necessary to consult with the accounting or cost accounting department. In this case, a rough figure of financial loss per defective will be sufficient. Replacing the number of defectives or percentages with the financial loss figures is a recommended way of making a Pareto diagram. Remember that sometimes a large number of defectives may not represent a great amount of money lost while on the other hand sometimes a small number of defectives may represent a great deal of money lost.

Chapter 6

Graphs

6.1 What is a graph?

When we visit companies and are shown around their factories, we see that nearly all of them use graphs. We are given various explanations with graphs before our eyes. But are these graphs being fully utilized as a tool for management? Here are three questions for you to attempt to answer:

1) What is the purpose of the graph?

2) How are these graphs used?

3) How can the graphs be made more useful?

Could you answer these questions? I have found in the past that most people couldn't. They would reply that graphs are troublesome, difficult, that they have not yet learned about them in QC education, that they use higher level statistical methods, etc. But, as a matter of fact, primary school children in the fourth grade already know the basic principles and methods of making graphs. Let's review some of the graphs that fourth-graders study and see how we can apply them in our jobs.

6.2 Various graphs

Let's concentrate on line graphs, bar graphs and pie charts. We'll compare the graphs taught in the fourth grade with those that factory foremen should make use of in their job.

(1) Line graphs (broken line graphs, curved line graphs)

Fourth grade graph	Factory foreman's graph
1 Broken line graph *a* The water is being heated. Check the temperature every five minutes and plot the results. ![Figure 6.1] **Figure 6.1** **Increase of water temperature**	*1* Broken line graph (transition graph) ![Figure 6.2] **Figure 6.2 Production amount by group**

51

On the basis of figure 6.1, put the corresponding temperatures in the table below.

Time (')	Temperature (°)
5-10	
10-15	
15-20	
20-25	
25-30	

b Connect the correct answer with the proper line graph as shown in **Figure 6.4**

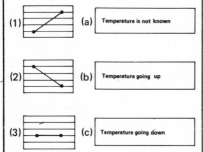

(1) (a) Temperature is not known

(2) (b) Temperature going up

(3) (c) Temperature going down

2 Curved line graph

Make a graph of the temperature every hour of the day.

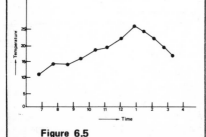

Figure 6.5

According to figure 6.5, what time was the lowest temperature and what time was the highest temperature? What was the difference in temperature between the two?

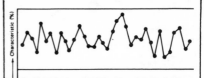

Figure 6.3 Manufacturing efficiency

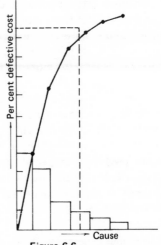

Figure 6.6

Many people probably think of something like the above when they hear the word 'graph.' Usually there is a horizontal and a vertical axis showing characteristic values related to both axes, and the points which are joined to make a line are determined on the basis of data showing both values. Graphs where the points are connected by a curved line are called curved line graphs and those connected by a broken line are called broken line graphs. Quality control charts have the date, time and order plotted on them and can be called special broke line graphs.

(2) Bar graphs (charts showing columns)

Fourth grade graph	Factory foreman's graph
1 Find the number of people working in different jobs in town and make a bar graph. *a* How many people does the first bar in figure 6.7 represent? *b* About how many persons are there in each occupation? Company employees Store employees Farmers Others *c* What fraction of company employees do the number of farmers represent?	By comparing the relative lengths of the bars on bar graphs we can learn the relationship between the various amounts represented. In other words, unlike line graphs, bar graphs are used when the two characteristic values are not considered continuous, i.e. there is one characteristic value and the other is the description of it.

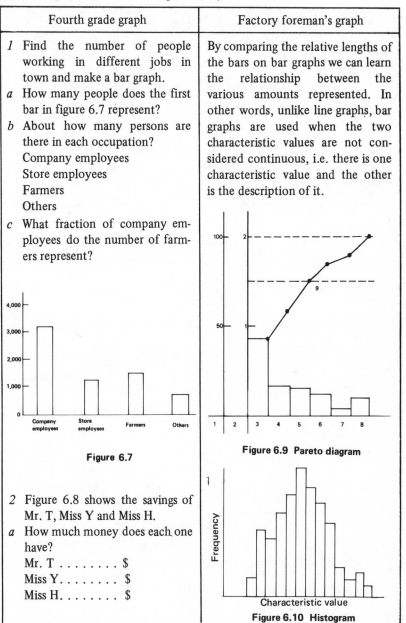

Figure 6.7

Figure 6.9 Pareto diagram

2 Figure 6.8 shows the savings of Mr. T, Miss Y and Miss H.

a How much money does each one have?

Mr. T . . . . $

Miss Y. . . . . $

Miss H. . . . . $

Figure 6.10 Histogram

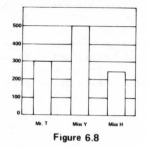

Figure 6.8

b How much more money does Miss Y have than Mr. T?

c What fraction of Miss Y's money does the amount of money of Miss H represent?

The size of each item is represented by the length or height of its bar. In quality control, the fraction defective, number of defectives and financial loss caused by the defectives for each defective item can be indicated in the Pareto diagram. Histograms can also be made not by listing the defective items along the horizontal axis but by dividing each characteristic value into classes and then showing the frequency of each one by the height of the bar.

(3) Pie charts

Fourth grade graph	Factory foreman's graph
1 Figure 6.11 shows the land usage in a certain town	*1* Pie charts

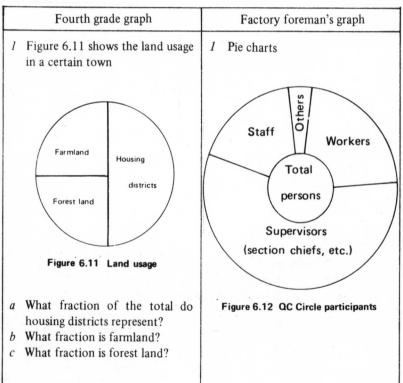

Figure 6.11 Land usage

Figure 6.12 QC Circle participants

a What fraction of the total do housing districts represent?

b What fraction is farmland?

c What fraction is forest land?

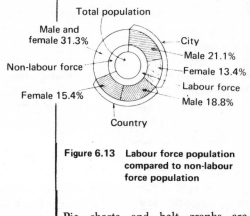

Total population

Male and
female 31.3%

Non-labour force

Female 15.4%

City
Male 21.1%
Female 13.4%
Labour force
Male 18.8%

Country

**Figure 6.13   Labour force population
compared to non-labour
force population**

In the fourth grade the students learn to make circle graphs within the limits of the decimal system, and in the fifth they learn to make pie charts taking in the concept of percentage through the use of a protractor.

Pie charts and belt graphs are used to indicate the operating rate of a factory, the number of workers involved in a job, the relationship of the part to the whole, the share of components, etc. Pie charts and belt graphs show the relationship in percentages and degrees.

(4) How to use and read graphs

So far we have been discussing the essential aspects of the various kinds of graphs. In this section, I have noted the important points to bear in mind when using and reading graphs:

(1) Both tables and graphs (except pie charts) are composed of a horizontal axis and a vertical axis, so you must keep both of these elements in mind when reading a graph. Be sure that you understand what both represent and their relationship to each other. It is easier to read a graph correctly if you use a ruler or triangle.

(2) A bar graph shows very clearly quantities and relationships between them. When reading or making one, keep this feature in mind. Make certain you know what the vertical and horizontal axes represent and what units of measurement are on the graph. The value represented by the units varies with the contents of each graph. (The quantities in the graph are represented not by the scale line of value units but by the size of intervals between each scale markings.) When a bar on a bar graph falls between two

value units, be sure you know what value unit each marking represents and how big each unit is. Also, when large amounts are involved, graphs only show approximate values, so make certain you keep in mind the significant figures obtainable from the graph.

(3) Line graphs are good for showing changes in numerical amounts. Watch changes in the direction of the line. Some graphs contain two (or more) different lines in order to compare changes such as $\bar{x}$-R control charts. The important point in this type of graph is the relationship between the two lines.

(4) Tables and graphs show various numerical values in connection with the sizes, changes and so forth. To make them easy to read, values are given in approximate figures and unnecessary information is omitted. Don't forget this when reading or making graphs.

It is very important to know just why you are making a graph, how it is intended to use the graph, and the characteristics of the different types of graphs. For this reason it is essential that you devise and make graphs for use on the job on the basis of a thorough understanding of the important points about graphs.

6.3 Examples of use of graphs

The following will explain how graphs can be combined and used, based on the fundamental examples given on pages 51 to 55.

Various kinds of special graph paper, such as binomial probability paper, logarithmic paper and others can be used. But rather than take this up now, in this chapter we shall study line graphs, bar graphs and pie charts, which are most fundamental.

(1) Two vertical bar graphs

Bar graphs may have their bars running either vertically or horizontally, and the axis in both cases is divided into units according to the characteristics and nature of the information to be represented. In figure 6.14, the bars are vertical but there are also times when horizontal bars are more convenient.

Note that if the vertical dimension of a bar graph is not long enough, the graph will have poor balance and be difficult to use.

(2) Bar graphs and broken line graphs

By combining a bar graph and a broken line graph, we can obtain a graph such as the one in figure 6.15. If the points plotted for the broken line graph are put at the centre of the bars, the graph will look good.

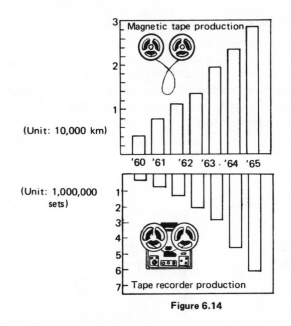

(Unit: 10,000 km)

(Unit: 1,000,000 sets)

Figure 6.14

To make the two graphs distinct, it is important to make the line connecting the plotted points thick and black. It is necessary to be very careful when making a graph containing compatible elements such as this one.

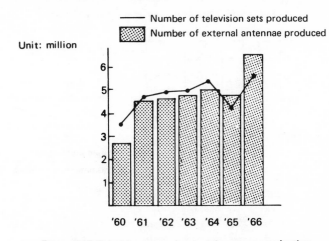

Unit: million

— Number of television sets produced

Number of external antennae produced

Figure 6.15 Television set and external antenna production

57

(3) Compound bar graphs and broken line graphs

To indicate changes in proportional composition, or changes over a period of time, segmented or compound bar graphs are used; to emphasize changes from one period of time to another, a broken line graph may be used. To minimize the confusion for someone looking at a compound bar graph, care must be taken with the hatching or other patterns used for each band (see figures 6.16, 6.17).

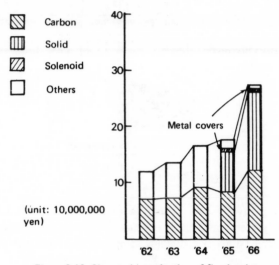

Figure 6.16 Changes in production of fixed resistors

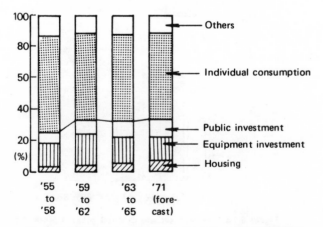

Figure 6.17 Structural changes in the gross national product

(4) Pie charts

Pie charts are most easily made when the circles are divided not into 360 degrees but into hundredths. When a pie chart is particularly complicated, a circle (or more than one circle) can be drawn within the circle of the pie proper (see figure 6.18). There are also half pie charts and other variations.

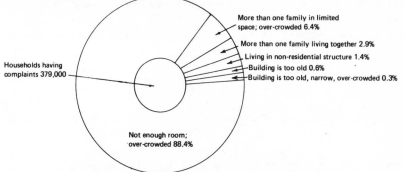

Figure 6.18 Causes for complaints about housing (in Osaka)

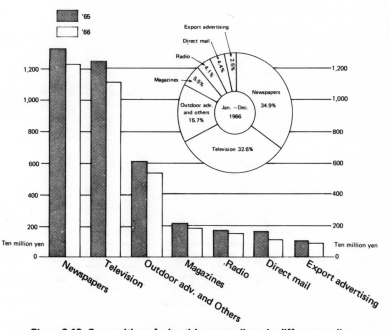

Figure 6.19 Composition of advertising expenditure in different media

59

(5) Bar graphs and pie charts

An interesting combination of two graphs may be obtained by combining a bar graph and a pie chart to show certain characteristics (in the bar graph portion of figure 6.19, growth in advertising expenditures in different media) and also the relative weight of each characteristic within the whole (proportional composition, in the pie chart in figure 6.19).

(6) Pictorial graphs

The advantage of pictorial graphs, such as the ones shown in figure 6.20, is that the symbols, which are placed at uniform, fixed intervals, visually contribute to the communication process.

Fundamental types of graphs, their use, and the key points in making them have been described so far, and it may be presumed that anyone in your company can make the graph he needs (to meet a specific purpose) by proceeding along the lines suggested. But when making a graph it is

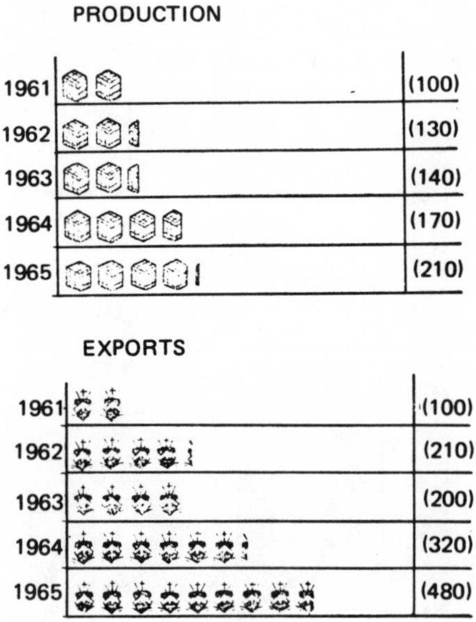

PRODUCTION

1961	◇◇	(100)
1962	◇◇▫	(130)
1963	◇◇▫	(140)
1964	◇◇◇◇	(170)
1965	◇◇◇◇▫	(210)

EXPORTS

1961	♔♔	(100)
1962	♔♔♔♔▫	(210)
1963	♔♔♔♔	(200)
1964	♔♔♔♔♔♔▫	(320)
1965	♔♔♔♔♔♔♔♔	(480)

Figure 6.20

essential to remember and understand that it is not sufficient for the person making the graph to understand it; it must be understood correctly by those who see it as well. If not, there is no purpose to making the graph. For the purpose of making a graph is to understand a situation quickly and take appropriate action.

6.4 From graphs to statistical control methods

As we have already mentioned, graphs have permeated our daily life in many ways. Now let us proceed from these graphs to more advanced methods.

Taking control charts as examples, we should recall the following points:

(1) The efficient use of graphs is essential. By using graphs, the past and present characteristics are made clear, and it is advisable to undertake stratification of data at this (i.e. the graph) stage. For proper analysis at this stage, it is important to fully utilize Pareto diagrams, cause-and-effect diagrams, histograms and pie charts.

(2) Statistical techniques are used for the transfer from graphs to control charts for process analysis. Statistical use is made of graphs by drawing control limit lines onto $\bar{x}$-R control charts, or c, p, or pn control charts. At this stage, a table which can be read at a glance may be usefully prepared from the control charts which indicate stratified, related characteristics.

(3) Finally, we come to the change from control charts made for process analysis to control charts made for process control. Since this is a particularly important stage, the control chart methodology as well as the various conditions imposed by the process in question must be fully and carefully studied. As regards the decision on whether to advance from control charts for process analysis to control charts for process control, please consult the following chapters on control charts.

Many points have been raised here, but I still recommend that you thoroughly master the basic concepts taught in the fourth grade in primary school before moving on to more advanced graphs.

Chapter 7

Control charts I

7.1 What is a control chart?

In the first chapter, we learned about the need for collecting data. In the following chapters we have studied ways of putting the data into order, by use of histograms and check sheets in which all the data are to be consolidated to show an overall picture, and Pareto diagrams which indicate problem areas. These methods group the data for a specified period and express them in a static form. However, in the plant we also want to know more about the nature of the changes that take place over a specified period of time, that is, the dynamic form. This means that we not only have to see what changes in data occur over time; we must also study the impact of the various factors in the process that change over time. Thus, if the materials, the workers, or the working methods or equipment were to change during this time, we would have to note the effect of such changes on production. One way of following these changes is by using graphs.

Figure 7.1 is a histogram based on data for synthetic resin parts collected five times a day (the values have been rounded off to make it easier to understand).

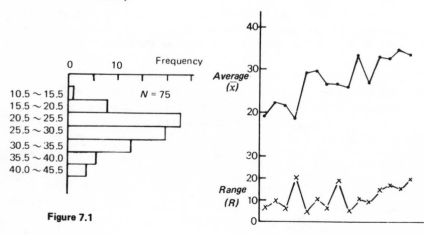

Figure 7.1

Figure 7.2

Using this data, a graph (figure 7.2) was drawn indicating the average daily value ($\bar{x}$) and daily range (R). It was drawn in the same way as the ordinary broken line graph (cf. p. 51). This graph shows that the values were low at the outset but showed a tendency to rise over time. We could not have learned that fact just by looking at the histogram in figure 7.1. In other words, we were able to obtain new information by looking at the movement of the data.

Now the problem is to find out whether the points on the graph are abnormal or not. For example, the first four points of $\bar{x}$ might be normal or below normal. Thus, when the standards of evaluation are not clear, one is liable to make arbitrary judgement or the one favourable to oneself and the graph cannot be meaningful. **When such irrational evaluations are made, necessary action may be "missed" or unsuitable action may be taken "in haste", thus causing confusion.** This will result in inappropriate conclusions being drawn, thus lowering quality and efficiency.

For this reason, we draw limit lines on the graphs to indicate the standards for evaluation. These lines will indicate the dispersion of data on a statistical basis and let us know when an abnormal situation occurs in production. If we add limit lines to figure 7.2, we obtain the graph in

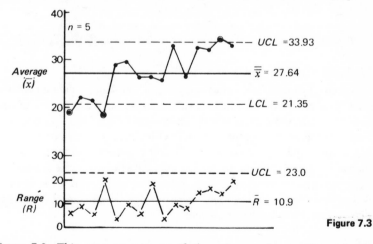

Figure 7.3

figure 7.3. This way we can see if there is any abnormality and take appropriate action. A graph or chart with limit lines is known as a **control chart**, and the lines are called control lines. There are three kinds of control lines: the upper control limit, the central line, and the lower control limit. They can be written as UCL, $\bar{\bar{x}}$ or $\bar{R}$, and LCL corresponding in the same order.

The purpose of drawing a control chart is to determine whether each of the points on the graph is normal or abnormal, and thus know the changes in the process from which the data has been collected. So each point on the graph must correctly indicate from which process the data were drawn.

For example, **in making control charts, the daily data are averaged out in order to obtain an average value for that day. Each of these values then becomes a point on the control chart which represents the characteristics of that given day.** Or, **data may be taken on a lot-by-lot basis.** In this case, the data must be collected in such a way that the point represents the given lot.

The points on a control chart represent arbitrary divisions in the manufacturing process. The data broken down into these divisions are referred to as sub-groups. In figure 7.3, the five measurements made in one day constitute one sub-group. In other words, we have divided the production process into units of one day, daily production has been represented by points on a control chart, and we can now determine whether the process is in a "controlled state" or not.

The role of a group leader is to be fully aware of the characteristics within his purview and to take measures immediately when he detects any abnormality. Thus, in order to carry out his duties effectively, it is most important for him to make control charts by constituting these sub-groups.

7.2 Types of control charts

A control chart's form varies according to the kind of data it contains. Some data are based on measurements such as the measurement of unit parts (in mm), or yields of a chemical process (in g). These are known as 'indiscrete values' or 'continuous data'. Other data are based on counting, such as the number of defective articles or the number of defects. They are known as 'discrete values' or 'enumerated data'. Control charts based on these two categories of data will differ. Table 7.1 shows the kind of control chart to be used in each case, depending on whether it is based on indiscrete values or on discrete values.

Control charts can also be divided into two types according to their usage. As explained above, the control charts we use provide more information than mere data plotted in a chronological sequence: they indicate how **the influence of various factors** (such as materials, men, methods, etc) **changes over a period of time.** If two or more different factors are exerting an influence, we must stratify the data and draw up

Table 7.1 Types of data and control charts

Types of data		Control chart used
Indiscrete		
Examples:	measurements (1/100 mm) volume (cc) product weight (g) power consumed (kwh)	$\bar{x}\text{-}R$
Discrete		
Examples:	number of defectives	pn
	fraction defective	p
	second-class product rate	
Examples:	number of pin holes in pieces of plated sheet metal, differing in area; number of foreign particles in pharmaceutical compounds, differing in volumes (when the range in which the defects are possible, such as length, area, volume, etc, is not fixed)	u
	number of pin holes in a specified area; number of foreign particles in a specified volume (when the length, area, volume, etc is fixed)	c

separate charts so that each influence can be studied. For example, when two kinds of material are used, the differences in their characteristics can be seen clearly by having a separate chart for each material. In other words, we can examine the nature of these influences by stratifying the data in accordance with the process factors, or in some cases by changing the grouping method. This use of charts is called "process analysis".

Let us assume that the process analysis has been made and that a controlled state has been achieved. Standardization of working methods is necessary to maintain this state. A control chart with control limit lines enables us to see if this standardization was correct and whether it is being maintained. If it is, then all points on the chart thereafter should be within the control limit lines, which are extended from the controlled state. If points appear on the control chart outside these limits, then some change must have occurred on the assembly or manufacturing line. The cause must be investigated and proper action taken. This use of charts is called "process control" Charts for process analysis and charts for process control are made in the same way, but their purposes differ. The purpose of process analysis is to detect the causes of any dispersion in the process by separating charts for individual items or by changing grouping methods; the purpose of process control is to detect any abnormality in the process by plotting the data day-by-day.

7.3 Making the $\bar{x}$-R control chart

An $\bar{x}$-R control chart is one that shows both the mean value, $\bar{x}$, and the range, R. This is the most common type of control chart using indiscrete values. The $\bar{x}$ portion of the chart mainly shows any changes in the mean value of the process, while the R portion shows any changes in the dispersion of the process. This chart is particularly useful because it shows changes in mean value and dispersion of the process at the same time, making it a very effective method for checking abnormalities in the process (see table 7.2).

Table 7.2 $\bar{x}$-R control chart

Sub-group No.	6:00	10:00	14:00	18:00	22:00	$\bar{x}$	R
1	14.0	12.6	13.2	13.1	12.1	13.00	1.9
2	13.2	13.3	12.7	13.4	12.1	12.94	1.3
3	13.5	12.8	13.0	12.8	12.4	12.90	1.1
4	13.9	12.4	13.3	13.1	13.2	13.18	1.5
5	13.0	13.0	12.1	12.2	13.3	12.72	1.2
6	13.7	12.0	12.5	12.4	12.4	12.60	1.7
7	13.9	12.1	12.7	13.4	13.0	13.02	1.8
8	13.4	13.6	13.0	12.4	13.5	13.18	1.2
9	14.4	12.4	12.2	12.4	12.5	12.78	2.2
10	13.3	12.4	12.6	12.9	12.8	12.80	0.9
11	13.3	12.8	13.0	13.0	13.1	13.04	0.5
12	13.6	12.5	13.3	13.5	12.8	13.14	1.1
13	13.4	13.3	12.0	13.0	13.1	12.96	1.4
14	13.9	13.1	13.5	12.6	12.8	13.18	1.3
15	14.2	12.7	12.9	12.9	12.5	13.04	1.7
16	13.6	12.6	12.4	12.5	12.2	12.66	1.4
17	14.0	13.2	12.4	13.0	13.0	13.12	1.6
18	13.1	12.9	13.5	12.3	12.8	12.92	1.2
19	14.6	13.7	13.4	12.2	12.5	13.28	2.4
20	13.9	13.0	13.0	13.2	12.6	13.14	1.3
21	13.3	12.7	12.6	12.8	12.7	12.82	0.7
22	13.9	12.4	12.7	12.4	12.8	12.84	1.5
23	13.2	12.3	12.6	13.1	12.7	12.78	0.9
24	13.2	12.8	12.8	12.3	12.6	12.74	0.9
25	13.3	12.8	13.0	12.3	12.2	12.72	1.1

$$\Sigma\bar{x} = 323.50 \qquad \Sigma R = 33.8$$

$$\bar{\bar{x}} = 12.940 \qquad \bar{R} = 1.35$$

Here are the steps for making the $\bar{x}$-R control chart.

Step 1. Collect the data. You usually need more than 100 samples. They should be taken from recent data from a process similar to the one that will be used thereafter.

Step 2. Put the data into sub-groups. These sub-groups can be according to measurement or lot order and should include from two to five samples each. The data should be divided into sub-groups in keeping with the following conditions:

a the data obtained under the same technical conditions should form a sub-group;

b a sub-group should not include data from a different lot or of a different nature.

For this reason, data are usually divided into sub-groups according to date, time, lot, etc. The number of samples in a sub-group determines the size of the sub-group and is represented by n; the number of sub-groups is represented by k.

Step 3. Record the data on a data sheet. The data sheet should be so designed that it is easy to compute the values of $\bar{x}$ and R for each sub-group. Table 7.2 gives data on the moisture content of a textile product, taken five times a day. Here $n = 5$ and $k = 25$.

Step 4. Find the mean value, $\bar{x}$. Use the following formula for each sub-group. Compute the mean value $\bar{x}$ to one decimal beyond that of the original measurement value.

$$\bar{x} = \frac{x_1 + x_2 + x_3 \ldots + x_n}{n}$$

For the data in sub-group No. 1, it works out like this:

$$\bar{x} = \frac{14.0 + 12.6 + 13.2 + 13.1 + 12.1}{5} = \frac{65.0}{5}$$
$$= 13.00$$

And for No. 2,

$$\bar{x} = \frac{13.2 + 13.3 + 12.7 + 13.4 + 12.1}{5} = \frac{64.7}{5}$$
$$= 12.94$$

Step 5. Find the range, R. Use the following formula to compute the range R for each sub-group:

$$R = x_{(\text{largest value})} - x_{(\text{smallest value})}$$

67

For sub-groups No. 1 and No. 2 in Table 7.2, R works out to:

$$R = 14.0 - 12.1 = 1.9$$
$$R = 13.4 - 12.1 = 1.3$$

Step 6. Find the overall mean, $\bar{\bar{x}}$. Total the mean values $\bar{x}$, for each sub-group and divide by the number of sub-groups k.

Thus, $\bar{\bar{x}} = \dfrac{\bar{x}_1 + \bar{x}_2 + \bar{x}_3 \ldots + \bar{x}_n}{k}$

Compute the overall mean value $\bar{\bar{x}}$ to two decimals beyond that of the original measurement value. For the data on Table 7.2 it works out like this:

$$\bar{\bar{x}} = \frac{13.0 + 12.94 + 12.90 \ldots + 12.72}{25} = \frac{323.50}{25}$$
$$= 12.940$$

Step 7. Compute the average value of the range $\bar{R}$. Total R for all groups and divide by the number of sub-groups, k. Thus,

$$\bar{R} = \frac{R_1 + R_2 + R_3 \ldots + R_k}{k}$$

Compute the average value $\bar{R}$ to one decimal beyond that of R. R for the data in Table 7.2 works out to:

$$\bar{R} = \frac{1.9 + 1.3 + 1.1 \ldots + 1.1}{25} = \frac{33.8}{25}$$
$$= 1.35$$

Step 8. Compute the control limit lines. Use the following formulas for $\bar{x}$ and R control charts. However, the coefficients A_2, D_4, D_3 etc are shown in Table 7.3.

Table 7.3

n	A_2	D_4	D_3
2	1.880	3.267	
3	1.023	2.575	
4	0.729	2.282	Do not apply
5	0.577	2.115	
6	0.483	2.004	
7	0.419	1.924	0.076

$\bar{x}$ control charts:

Central line CL = $\bar{\bar{x}}$;
Upper control limit UCL = $\bar{\bar{x}} + A_2\bar{R}$;
Lower control limit LCL = $\bar{\bar{x}} - A_2\bar{R}$.

R control charts:

Central line CL = $\bar{R}$;
Upper control limit UCL = $D_4\bar{R}$;
Lower control limit LCL = $D_3\bar{R}$.

For the data on Table 7.2, this works out as:

$$
\begin{aligned}
\bar{x} \text{ control chart CL} &= \bar{\bar{x}} = 12.940 \\
\text{UCL} &= \bar{\bar{x}} + A_2\bar{R} \\
&= 12.940 + 0.577 \times 1.35 \\
&= 12.940 + 0.779 \\
&= 13.719 \\
\text{LCL} &= \bar{\bar{x}} - A_2\bar{R} \\
&= 12.940 - 0.577 \times 1.35 \\
&= 12.161 \\
R \text{ control chart CL} &= \bar{R} = 1.35 \\
\text{UCL} &= D_4\bar{R} \\
&= 2.115 \times 1.35 \\
&= 2.86 \\
\text{LCL} &= D_3\bar{R} \text{ (none)}
\end{aligned}
$$

Step 9. Construct the control chart. Obtain graph paper or control chart paper and set the index so that the upper and lower control limits will be separated by 20 to 30 mm. Draw in the control lines and the numerical values. The central line is a solid line and limit lines for process analysis are broken lines, while limit lines for process control are dotted lines.

Step 10. Plot out the $\bar{x}$ and R points for each sub-group on the same vertical line. Plot the $\bar{x}$ and R values as computed for each sub-group. For the $\bar{x}$ values use a dot (.) and for the R values use an (x). Circle all points which exceed the control limit lines to distinguish them from the others. The dots and the x's should be about 2 to 5 mm apart. Figure 7.4 shows a control chart based on the data in table 7.2.

69

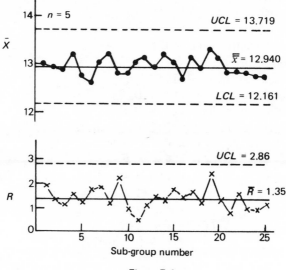

Figure 7.4

Step 11. Write in the necessary information. On the left edge of the control chart write $\bar{x}$ and R, and on the upper left of an $\bar{x}$ control chart write the n value. Also indicate the nature of the data, the period when it was taken, the instruments used, the person responsible, etc.

Chapter 8

Control charts II

8.1 Point movements on $\bar{x}$-R control charts

In chapter 7, we saw how to make $\bar{x}$-R control charts, and in the practice exercises we learned that we can use $\bar{x}$-R control charts to understand changes in a production process.

Before we can actually use a control chart, however, we must know the following things:

    a the relationship between the change in the production process and the change (the movement of points) on the control chart;

    b the relationship between the degree of change in the production process and the degree of change (movement of points) on the control chart.

Let us try some experiments to learn more about this movement of points on the control chart.

Experiment 1

The total data for one day's production of a certain product serve as the basis for the histogram in figure 8.1. Let's call this 'distribution A'. Write the data on little chips, collect all the chips, and they should display the same distribution as A. Then put them in a large bowl so they can be mixed well (see figure 8.4).

The production process in this factory is stable and the quality of each day's products is represented by distribution A. Now, if we continue production in this manner and measure five ($n = 5$) samples at random each day, how would the resulting control chart appear?

71

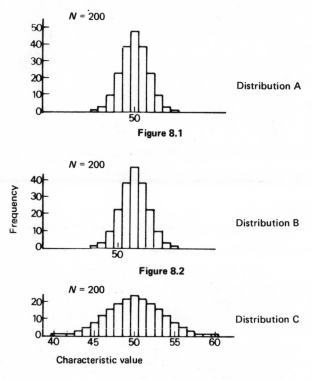

Distribution A

Figure 8.1

Distribution B

Figure 8.2

Distribution C

Figure 8.3

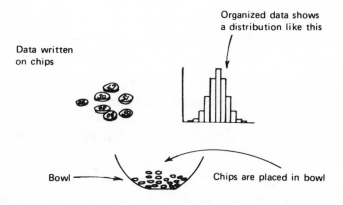

Organized data shows
a distribution like this

Data written
on chips

Bowl

Chips are placed in bowl

Figure 8.4 Distribution A of chips

It can be assumed that daily production continues to follow distribution A of figure 8.1. Therefore, take five of the A chips at random and use the data on them to work out your control chart. Take data for 25 days (sub-groups) from these chips (i.e., 5 pieces x 25 days = 125 pieces) and use this to construct an $\bar{x}$-R control chart. This chart will look like figure 8.5.

Information obtained from figure 8.5

As can be seen clearly from the control chart, although the production is controlled, $\bar{x}$ and R do show some fluctuation. However, they do not exceed the control limits and there does not seem to be any tendency for the values to assume a particular form.

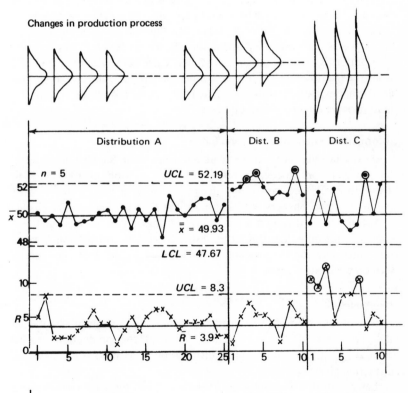

Figure 8.5   Figure 8.6   Figure 8.7

If this condition continues, the points on $\bar{x}$-R control charts based on five daily samples will continue to form the same curves shown here. Even if the control limit lines are extended, and points are drawn in based on the data from the distribution A chips, all points will still be within the control lines. There should also be no clustering. The state arising when the production process is stable and there is no abnormality in the points on the control chart is called a *controlled state*.

Experiment 2

When a factor (such as raw materials, machinery, working methods, workers, etc) changes and consequently the mean value of a characteristic of the product shows a slight change, what change will there be in the points on the control chart? Let's assume that distribution A had made a 'plus' movement to the right as in figure 8.2. This distribution will be referred to as B. The data are written on little chips which, when collected, should display the same distribution B. If production is continued as represented by distribution B, we can take the data from the distribution B chips to obtain the process data. Let's take ten days' data from the distribution B chips, at five per day. If we make an $\bar{x}$-R control chart on this basis, it will appear as in figure 8.6. We'll use the control limit lines we used for distribution A.

Information obtained from figure 8.6

As can be seen clearly from figure 8.6, when there is a shift in the mean for a production process (in other words, a shift from distribution A to distribution B), you can readily detect a change in the $\bar{x}$ control chart. In this case, no changes can be seen on the R control chart. The change in the mean of the production process brings about changes in the $\bar{x}$ control chart only. The shift from distribution A to distribution B was a very small one for the production process, but a clear difference can be seen on the control chart.

Experiment 3

Now, let us see what happens to the points on the control chart when the dispersion of the characteristic value of the production process changes. We'll leave the mean at distribution A as it was but make the dispersion greater (figure 8.3).

Let us call this distribution C. Prepare chips in the same manner as we did before so that they will, all together, show distribution C. As in experiment 2, take ten days' data from distribution C at $n = 5$. Continuing on the same control chart as before, the points will appear as in figure 8.7.

Information obtained from figure 8.7

When the dispersion of the production process changes, points on the R control chart show abnormality. Also note that the spread of the points on the $\bar{x}$ control chart becomes greater and some go beyond the control limits.

Conclusion

The results of the experiments are, finally, that a change in the mean for the production process will result in an abnormality appearing on the $\bar{x}$ control chart. When the mean of the production process shifts to the plus side, the points on the $\bar{x}$ control chart will also move to the plus side. Even when the change in the mean of the production process is very slight, the points on the control chart will react appreciably to this change.

Secondly, a change in the dispersion for the production process, on the other hand, results in abnormalities appearing on both the $\bar{x}$ and R control charts. When the dispersion of the production process increases, the points on the R control chart will tend to increase as well. Moreover, the points on the $\bar{x}$ control chart will display a greater spread and there will be cases where the points may go beyond the control limits.

These results can be summarized as in table 8.1.

Table 8.1

Type of chart	Change in the mean of production process	Change of the dispersion
$\bar{x}$ control chart	indicates abnormality	indicates abnormality
R control chart	—	indicates abnormality

The experiments we have just conducted show the movement of points on control charts when there is a change in the production process. In practice, however, we use this the other way around: on the basis of movements of the points on the control chart, we want to see what changes have taken place in the production process. It is thus important that you practise this repeatedly so you can guess what changes have occurred in the production process, as indicated on the upper part of figure 8.5, 8.6 and 8.7, by looking at the movement of the points on the control charts.

75

8.2 How to read control charts

As stated above, the purpose of making a control chart is to determine, on the basis of the movements of the points, what kind of changes have taken place in the production process. Therefore, to use the control chart effectively, we have to set the criteria for evaluating what we consider an abnormality. When a production process is in a controlled state, as shown in figure 8.5, this means that:

    1. All points lie within the control limits, and

    2. The point grouping does not form a particular form.

We would therefore know that an abnormality has developed if

    a) Some points are outside the control limits (including points on the limit lines), or

    b) The points form some sort of particular form even though they are all within the control limits.

The situation is obvious when some of the points are outside the limits, so let us rather concentrate on the above (b) case and set up more detailed standards.

Non-randomness and its evaluation

A. Runs When points line up on one side only of the central line (strictly speaking, the median line), this is called a 'run.' The number of points in that run is called the 'length of the run' (see figure 8.8). In evaluating runs, if the run has a length of 7 points, we conclude that there is an abnormality in the process. Even with a run of less than 6, if 10 out of 11 points or 12 out of 14 points lie on one side, we consider there is an abnormality in the production process. On $\bar{x}$ control charts, the central line and the median line almost correspond, but on R control charts or on p, pn, c and u control charts the proper procedure is to draw in the median line and then evaluate.

B. Trends If there is a continued rise or fall in a series of points, we say there is a 'trend' (see figure 8.9). In evaluating trends, we consider that if 7 consecutive points continue to rise or fall there is an abnormality. Often, however, the points will go beyond the control limits before reaching 7.

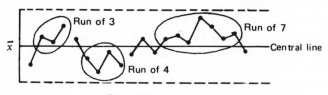

Figure 8.8 Runs

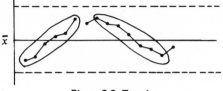

Figure 8.9 Trend

C. Periodicity If the points show the same pattern of change (for example, rise or fall) over equal intervals, we say there is 'periodicity' (see figure 8.10). When it comes to evaluating periodicity, there is no simple method as with runs and trends. The only way is to follow the point movement closely and make a technical decision.

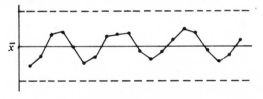

Figure 8.10 Periodicity

D. Hugging of the control line When the points on the control chart stick close to the central line or to the control limit line, we speak of 'hugging of the control line'. Often, in this situation, a different type of data or data from different factors have been mixed into the sub-group. It is therefore necessary to change the sub-grouping, reassemble the data and redraw the control chart. For evaluation, in order to decide whether or not there is hugging of the central line, draw two lines on the control chart, one of them between the central line and the UCL and the other between the central line and the LCL. If most of the points lie between these two lines, there is an abnormality (see figure 8.11). To see whether

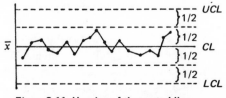

Figure 8.11 Hugging of the central line

77

there is hugging of the control limit lines, two lines should be drawn at two-thirds of the distance between the central line and control line, from the central line, as in figure 8.12. There is abnormality if 2 out of 3 points, 3 out of 7 points, or 4 out of 10 points lie within the outer one-third zone (see figure 8.12).

Figure 8.12 Hugging of the control limit lines

8.3 How to draw *p* and *pn* control charts

A *p* chart is one that shows the fraction defective (*p*), whereas a *pn* chart shows the number of defectives (*pn*). Basically, they are the same except that a *pn* chart is used when the size of the sub-group (*n*) is constant and a *p* chart is used when it is not constant. The *p* and *pn* charts are not used together as are the $\bar{x}$-R control charts. This is because *p* and *pn* charts show the characteristics of both the mean and the dispersion of the production process.

First let us see how to construct a *p* chart. Then, for the *pn* chart, the method for finding the control line will be explained.

(1) p chart

Step 1. Collect the data. Get as much data as you can which tell you the number inspected (*n*) and the number of defective products (*pn*) You will need at least 20 pairs (see table 8.2).

Step 2. Divide the data into sub-groups. Usually, the data are grouped by date or lots. The sub-group size (*n*) should be over 50 and the mean value of defectives for each sub-group should range from 3 to 4. Table 8.2 shows fraction defective for electric machines grouped by lots.

Table 8.2 Fraction defective for electric machine parts

Sub-group No.	Sub-group size n	Number of defectives pn	Per cent defective p (%)	UCL (%)	LCL (%)
1	115	15	13.0	18.8	1.8
2	220	18	8.2	16.5	4.1
3	210	23	11.0	16.6	4.0
4	220	22	10.0	16.5	4.1
5	220	18	8.2	16.5	4.1
6	255	15	5.9	16.0	4.6
7	440	44	10.0	14.6	6.0
8	365	47	12.9	15.1	5.5
9	255	13	5.1	16.0	4.6
10	300	33	11.0	15.6	5.0
11	280	42	15.0	15.8	4.8
12	330	46	13.9	15.3	5.3
13	320	38	11.9	16.5	4.1
14	225	29	12.9	16.4	4.2
15	290	26	9.0	15.7	4.9
16	170	17	10.0	17.3	3.3
17	65	5	7.7	21.6	0
18	100	7	7.0	19.4	1.2
19	135	14	10.4	18.2	2.4
20	280	36	12.9	15.8	4.8
21	250	25	10.0	16.1	4.5
22	220	24	10.9	16.5	4.1
23	220	20	9.1	16.5	4.1
24	220	15	6.8	16.5	4.1
25	220	18	8.2	16.5	4.1
Total	5925	610			
Total					

Step 3. Compute the fraction defective for each sub-group and enter it on a data sheet. Use a data sheet which resembles table 8.2. To find the fraction defective, use the following formula:

$$p = \frac{\text{number of defectives}}{\substack{\text{size of sub-group} \\ \text{(number inspected} \\ \text{in sub-group)}}} = \frac{pn}{n}$$

To indicate as a percentage, multiply by 100.

Step 4. Find the average fraction defective

$$\bar{p} = \frac{\text{Total defectives}}{\text{Total inspected}} = \frac{\Sigma pn}{\Sigma n}$$

for table 8.2 this works out to:

$$\bar{p} = \frac{\Sigma pn}{\Sigma n} = \frac{610}{5925} = 0.103 \ (= 10.3\%)$$

Step 5. Compute the control limits.

Central line: CL = $\bar{p}$ = 10.3 (%)

Upper control limit:

$$\text{UCL} = \bar{p} + 3 \sqrt{\frac{\bar{p}(1 - \bar{p})}{n}} = \bar{p} + \frac{3}{\sqrt{n}} \sqrt{\bar{p}(1 - \bar{p})}$$

$$= 0.103 + \frac{3}{\sqrt{n}} \times 0.304$$

Lower control limit:

$$\text{LCL} = \bar{p} - 3 \sqrt{\frac{\bar{p}(1 - \bar{p})}{n}}$$

$$= 0.103 - \frac{3}{\sqrt{n}} \times 0.304$$

Remember that the value of the control limits will change depending on the size of the sub-group, (*n*). Therefore, on the control chart, the control limit lines will show some variations. To make it easier to compute the control limits, there are tables which give you the $\frac{3}{\sqrt{n}}$ value for a given *n* and the $\sqrt{\bar{p}(1 - \bar{p})}$ value for a given $\bar{p}$. (In Japan, such tables are available from the Japan Industrial Standards Association, *JIS Z-9021, Control Chart Methods,* and from the JUSE, *the Nikkagiren Numerical Values Table A.)*

Step 6. Draw in the control lines and plot *p*. The control chart based on the data in table 8.2 will look like figure 8.13.

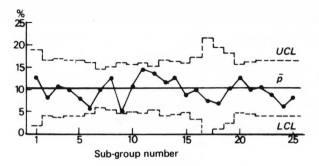

Figure 8.13 *p* control chart

(2) pn chart

Table 8.3 provides data on electroplating part defectives on the basis of lots. The lot size is set at 100 so the *pn* chart can be made. The tables mentioned above can be used to find the control limit values ($3\sqrt{\bar{p}n}$ from a given $\bar{p}n$ and $\sqrt{1-\bar{p}}$ from a given $\bar{p}$.)

Table 8.3 Plating defects of assembled parts

Sub-group No.	Sub-group size n	Number of defectives pn	Sub-group No.	Sub-group size n	Number of defectives pn
1	100	1	16	100	5
2	''	6	17	''	4
3	''	5	18	''	1
4	''	5	19	''	6
5	''	4	20	''	15
6	''	3	21	''	12
7	''	2	22	''	6
8	''	2	23	''	3
9	''	4	24	''	4
10	''	6	25	''	3
11	''	2	26	''	3
12	''	1	27	''	2
13	''	3	28	''	5
14	''	1	29	''	7
15	''	4	30	''	4
			Total	3000	129
			Average	100	4.3

($\bar{p}$ = 129/3000 = 0.043)

81

Central line: CL = $\bar{p}n$ = 129/30 = 4.30

Upper control limit:

$$UCL = \bar{p}n + 3\sqrt{\bar{p}n(1 - \bar{p})}$$
$$= \bar{p}n + 3\sqrt{\bar{p}n}\sqrt{1 - \bar{p}}$$
$$= 4.30 + (6.22)(0.98) = 4.30 + 6.09 = 10.39$$

Lower control limit:

$$LCL = \bar{p}n - 3\sqrt{\bar{p}n(1 - \bar{p})}$$
$$= \bar{p}n - 3\sqrt{\bar{p}n}\sqrt{1 - \bar{p}}$$
$$= 4.30 - 6.09 \quad \text{(no consideration due to negative}$$
$$\text{value)}$$

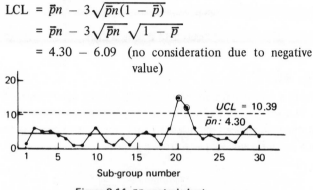

Figure 8.14 *pn* **control chart**

Figure 8.14 is the *pn* chart made on the basis of the data shown in table 8.3.

8.4 How to make *u* charts and *c* charts

A *u* control chart is used in dealing with number of defectives such as the unevenness of woven materials or pin holes in enamel wire, and when the material being inspected is not constant in area and length. A *c* control chart is used in dealing with the number of defects which appear in fixed unit samples, such as the number of imperfectly soldered connections in radios, etc.

First let us look at the necessary steps for drawing a *u* chart. Then we will explain now to find the control limits for a *c* chart.

(1) u control chart

Step 1. Collect the data. Collect as much data as you can which tells you number of units *n* and number of defects *c*. For example, let's assume there is a 5m^2 electroplated copper plate with eight pin holes in it. One unit will be 1m^2 so *n* = 5, and *c* = 8.

Step 2. Group the data. Do this by lots, products, or samples, etc. Fix the sub-group size so that u will be larger than 2 or 3. Table 8.4 shows data on pin holes in enamel wire.

Table 8.4 Number of pinholes in enamel wire

Sub-group No	Sub-group size n	No. of pinholes c	No. of pinholes per unit u	$\frac{1}{\sqrt{n}}$	UCL $\bar{u} + 3\sqrt{\bar{u}} \times \frac{1}{\sqrt{n}}$	LCL $\bar{u} - 3\sqrt{\bar{u}} \times \frac{1}{\sqrt{n}}$
1	1.0	4	4.0	1	8.10	—
2	1.0	5	5.0	1	8.10	—
3	1.0	3	3.0	1	8.10	—
4	1.0	3	3.0	1	8.10	—
5	1.0	5	5.0	1	8.10	—
6	1.3	2	1.5	0.877	7.07	—
7	1.3	5	3.8	0.877	7.07	—
8	1.3	3	2.3	0.877	7.07	—
9	1.3	2	1.5	0.877	7.07	—
10	1.3	1	0.8	0.877	7.07	—
11	1.3	5	3.8	0.877	7.07	—
12	1.3	2	1.5	0.877	7.07	—
13	1.3	4	3.1	0.872	7.07	—
14	1.3	2	1.5	0.877	7.07	—
15	1.2	6	5.0	0.913	7.65	—
16	1.2	4	3.3	0.913	7.65	—
17	1.2	0	0	0.913	7.65	—
18	1.7	8	4.7	0.767	6.90	—
19	1.7	3	1.8	0.767	6.90	—
20	1.7	8	4.7	0.767	6.90	—

Total $\Sigma n = 25.4$ $\Sigma c = 75$

Step 3. Find the number of defects per unit for each sub-group and then compute u.

Find u with the following formula:

$$u = \frac{\text{number of defects per sub-group } (c)}{\text{number of units per sub-group } (n)} = \frac{c}{n}$$

Find $\bar{u}$ with the following formula:

$$\bar{u} = \frac{\text{total defects for all sub-groups}}{\text{total units for all sub-groups}} = \frac{\Sigma c}{\Sigma n}$$

$\bar{u}$ for the data in table 8.4 works out to:

$$\bar{u} = \frac{75}{25.4} \fallingdotseq 2.95$$

Step 4. Compute the control limits.

Central line: CL = $\bar{\bar{u}}$ = 2.95

Upper control limit: UCL = $\bar{\bar{u}} + 3\sqrt{\dfrac{\bar{\bar{u}}}{n}} = \bar{\bar{u}} + \dfrac{3\sqrt{\bar{\bar{u}}}}{\sqrt{n}}$

$$= 2.95 + \dfrac{5.15}{\sqrt{n}}$$

Lower control limit: LCL = $\bar{\bar{u}} - 3\sqrt{\dfrac{\bar{\bar{u}}}{n}} = \bar{\bar{u}} - \dfrac{3\sqrt{\bar{\bar{u}}}}{\sqrt{n}}$

$$= 2.95 - \dfrac{5.15}{\sqrt{n}}$$

Here, too, the limit values change according to the value of *n*. Also the table mentioned above (from JIS, JUSE or other sources) will give you the value of $3\sqrt{\bar{\bar{u}}}$ for a given *u* and $\sqrt{1/n}$ for a given *n*.

Step 5. Draw in the control lines and plot *u*. A chart made on the basis of the data in table 8.4 would appear as figure 8.15.

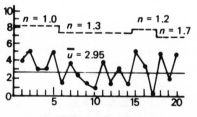

Sub-group number

Figure 8.15 *u* **control chart**

(2) c control chart

Table 8.5 shows data on the number of defects in woven material. The sample size is fixed at lm so a *c* chart can be made. The following formula is used to compute the control lines. (Here, too, use the tables to find the $3\sqrt{\bar{c}}$ value for a given $\bar{c}$.)

Central line: CL = $\bar{c}$ = 82/20 = 4.1

Upper control limit: UCL = $\bar{c} + 3\sqrt{\bar{c}}$

$$= 4.1 + 3\sqrt{4.1}$$

$$= 10.17$$

Lower control limit: LCL = $\bar{c} - 3\sqrt{\bar{c}}$

$$= 4.1 - 6.07$$

$$= -1.97 \text{ (no consideration due to negative value)}$$

A control chart based on the data from table 8.5 is shown in figure 8.16.

Table 8.5 Defects per square metre of fabric

Sample number	Number of defects	Sample number	Number of defects
1	7	11	6
2	5	12	3
3	3	13	2
4	4	14	7
5	3	15	2
6	8	16	4
7	2	17	7
8	3	18	4
9	4	19	2
10	3	20	3
		Total	82

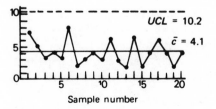

Figure 8.16 c control chart

8.5 How to use control charts

The following, basic steps should be taken for using control charts of the production process.

1 Select the items which should be controlled. First decide which problems are to be dealt with and for what purpose. On the basis of this decision, it should be clear what data will be needed.

2 Decide which control chart to use. Determine whether the $\bar{x}$-R, *p*, *pn*, *u*, or *c* chart is appropriate.

3 Make a control chart for process analysis. Take data for a certain period of time or use data from the past in making the chart. If any points are abnormal, investigate the cause and take action. The cause of the change in quality is studied by rearranging the sub-grouping, stratified data, and so on.

4 Construct a control chart for process control. Assume that action has been taken to deal with the cause of the quality change and the production process is controlled. Now see if the product satisfies the standards for this state. On the basis of these conclusions, standardize the working methods (or reform them if needed). Extend the control lines of the chart at stable situation and continue plotting the daily data.

5 Control the production process. If the standardized working methods are being maintained, the control chart should show this controlled state. If an abnormality appears on the chart, investigate the cause immediately and take proper action.

6 Recompute the control lines. If the equipment or the working methods are changed, the control lines must be recomputed. If control over the production process is accomplished smoothly, the quality level of the control chart should keep improving. In this case, make periodic reviews of the control lines. The following rules should be observed in recomputing the control lines:

  i. Data on points which indicate an abnormality and for which the cause has been found and corrected should not be included in recomputing;

  ii. Data on abnormal points for which the cause cannot be found or no action can be taken should be included.

Control charts are easy to construct so they are widely used. But there are surprisingly few really useful charts. I hope that after studying this section, you will be able to draw control charts which are truly effective.

Chapter 9

Scatter diagrams

9.1 Relationship between cause and effect

Control charts are being introduced as part of the production process in factories. Once, when visiting a factory, I noticed a cause-and-effect diagram on the wall next to the control chart for a certain production process. I asked the foreman about this diagram, and he proudly replied: "I was only able to come up with ten causes on my own, whereas, when the members of the QC circle made an investigation, they were able to list as many as 40 items." I asked him whether he had studied the relationship between cause and effect. He replied: "We have made a rough study together, and I think it is firm, but I did not go so far as . . . " This means that at best he will have a list of "comprehended causes" or a list of "many causes," but the efforts of the QC circle members in revealing the causes are not being utilized sufficiently. One should also study the relationship between cause and effect, keeping the effective or related ones and dropping the ineffective or unrelated ones. If a new cause is found, add it to the list. It is only through this process that the cause-and-effect diagram can really have an impact (see figure 9.1). Of course, this foreman was well aware that just listing the causes meant nothing unless this was used, but he did not know how to study the relationship between the paired data. In all our studies until now, we have only handled one kind of data at a time. Now we are going to explain scatter diagrams which examine the relationship between the paired data. This will avoid the foregoing problem.

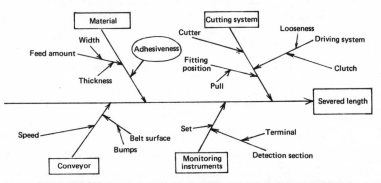

Figure 9.1 (A) Cause-and-effect diagram with all possible causes listed

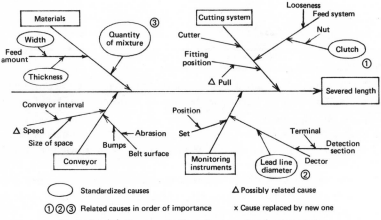

Figure 9.1 (B) Cause-and-effect diagram after further study

9.2 What is a scatter diagram?

Generally, when we talk about the relationship between two kinds of data we are actually talking about either (1) a cause-and-effect relationship, (2) a relationship between one cause and another, or (3) a relationship between one cause and two causes. For example, the relationship between moisture content in threads and elongation, the relationship between an ingredient and product hardness, the relationship between the cutting speed and variations in length of parts, the relationship between illumination levels and inspection mistakes, etc. Table 9.1 gives data on thread moisture content and elongation. If we use the vertical axis for elongation and the horizontal axis for moisture content, and then plot the data, we will make a diagram similar to figure 9.2. From this chart we can see that when the moisture content is greater the elongation is larger.

This kind of chart is called a scatter diagram. In this case, the moisture content and elongation values for 50 threads were necessary; for sample No. 1 the paired data turned out to be 1.5 per cent moisture content and 8.5 per cent elongation. The group of data collected from the same sample form a unit (as in this example) known as 'corresponding data'. Therefore, with a scatter diagram, several corresponding groups of data are collected and the two kinds of data are indexed and then plotted on an ordinary graph.

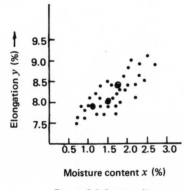

Figure 9.2 Scatter diagram

Table 9.1 Data sheet

Sample number	Moisture content x (%)	Elongation y (%)	Sample number	Moisture content x (%)	Elongation y (%)
1	1.5	8.5	20	1.9	8.6
2	1.3	8.1	21	1.6	8.1
3	1.9	8.3	22	1.7	8.2

Note: Lower position omitted

9.3 How to make a scatter diagram

Here is the procedure:

Step 1. Collect 50 to 100 paired samples of data whose relationship you wish to investigate, and enter them on a data sheet (see table 9.2).

Table 9.2 Data sheet

Number	Conveyor speed (cm/sec)	Severed length (mm)	Number	Conveyor speed (cm/sec)	Severed length (mm)
1	8.1	1046	26	8.0	1040
2	7.7	1030	27	5.5	1013
3	7.4	1039	28	6.9	1025
4	5.8	1027	29	7.0	1020
5	7.6	1028	30	7.5	1022
6	6.8	1025	31	6.7	1020
7	7.9	1035	32	8.1	1035
8	6.3	1015	33	9.0	1052
9	7.0	1038	34	7.1	1021
10	8.0	1036	35	7.6	1024
11	8.0	1026	36	8.5	1029
12	8.0	1041	37	7.5	1015
13	7.2	1029	38	8.0	1030
14	6.0	1010	39	5.2	1010
15	6.3	1020	40	6.5	1025
16	6.7	1024	41	8.0	1031
17	8.2	1034	42	6.9	1030
18	8.1	1036	43	7.6	1034
19	6.6	1023	44	6.5	1034
20	6.5	1011	45	5.5	1020
21	8.5	1030	46	6.0	1025
22	7.4	1014	47	5.5	1023
23	7.2	1030	48	7.6	1028
24	5.6	1016	49	8.6	1020
25	6.3	1020	50	6.3	1026

Note: This sheet shows the results of investigating the conveyor speed (cause) and the severed length (effect) as seen in figure 9.1.

Step 2. Draw the horizontal and vertical axes of the graph. Indicate the higher figures on the upper part of the vertical axis and to the right of the horizontal axis. If you make the length of both axes about the same, the diagram will be easier to read. If the relationship between the two kinds of data is that of cause-and-effect, the cause values are usually placed on the horizontal axis and the effect values on the vertical axis.

Step 3. Plot the data on a graph (see figure 9.3). If data values are repeated and fall on the same point, make concentric circles, two or three as needed. If you have a lot of data or if the data contain many of the same value, it is troublesome to plot each one, so make use of the technique for constructing histograms (chapter 2) and make a frequency table with a vertical and horizontal index. This is another kind of scatter diagram which is called a correlation table (see table 9.3).

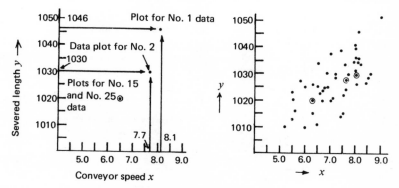

Figure 9.3 Plotting a scatter diagram

Table 9.3 Correlation table

		1	4	3	10	8	9	12	2	1	50
	1050									/	1
	1045							/			1
	1040					/	/	//			4
	1035				/		/	++++			7
Severed length y	1030					///	///	///	//		11
	1025		/	//	////	//	/	/			11
	1020		/		///	//	/				7
	1015		//		/		//				5
	1010	/		/	/						3
	1005										
		5.0	5.5	6.0	6.5	7.0	7.5	8.0	8.5	9.0	

Conveyor speed x

91

9.4 Reading scatter diagrams

If we look at figure 9.3 and table 9.3 we can see that as the conveyor speed increases, the length of the severed piece increases. The dispersion in the severed length for the same conveyor speeds is due to other causes. The correct reading of scatter diagrams must lead to proper action. To learn this correct reading ability we have shown samples of the most common scatter diagrams in figure 9.4. Here are some explanations.

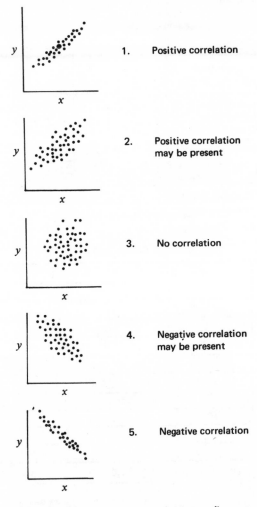

1. Positive correlation

2. Positive correlation may be present

3. No correlation

4. Negative correlation may be present

5. Negative correlation

Figure 9.4 Various plot patterns in scatter diagrams

1) An increase in *y* depends on increases in *x*. If *x* is controlled, *y* will be naturally controlled.

2) If *x* is increased, *y* will increase somewhat, but *y* seems to have causes other than *x*.

3) There is no correlation.

4) An increase in *x* will cause a tendency for decrease in *y*.

5) An increase in *x* will cause a decrease in *y*. Therefore, as with item 1 above, *x* may be controlled instead of *y*.

Note: Figures 9.2 and 9.4 should be examined according to the following rules.

9.5 Testing correlation with scatter diagrams

We have shown above how we can use scatter diagrams to determine the relationships between two kinds of data. But, when there is a correlation, how can we determine the extent of the correlation? The answer is that we can use either of two methods. One is to calculate the coefficient of correlation and the other method is based on a binomial probability paper (see chapter 10). Here we will touch upon the most practical one — the so-called median method for analyzing correlations.

1) Find the *x* median ($\tilde{x}$) and the *y* median ($\tilde{y}$). Draw both median lines on the scatter diagram (figure 9.5).

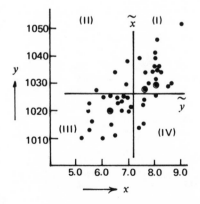

Figure 9.5 Drawing a median line

2) Mark the four areas made by the median lines I, II, III and IV, starting from the upper right and going counter-clockwise. Count the points in each area (table 9.4).

Table 9.4 Points in each area

Area	Points
(I)	19
(II)	4
(III)	20
(IV)	5
On the line	2
Total	50

3) Find the number of points for II and IV and N (total number of data minus number of points on the line). Number of points in II and IV is $4 + 5 = 9$, and $N = 50 - 2 = 48$.

4) Compare the total number of points in II and IV with the 'limit of number of points' column indicated in table 9.5. If the number of points of the two areas is less than the limited numbers, a correlation exists.

Table 9.5 Sign Test Table

N	Limit of number of Points for I + III, II + IV	N	Limit of number of Points for I + III, II + IV
20	5	42	14
21	5	44	15
22	5	46	15
23	6	48	16
24	6	50	17
25	7	52	18
26	7	54	19
27	7	56	20
28	8	58	21
29	8	60	21
30	9	62	22
32	9	64	23
34	10	66	24
36	11	68	25
38	12	70	26
40	13		

Note: This table is limited to $N = 20 - 70$ at a 5 per cent level of significance.

*Table 9.5 is a part of a Sign Test Table. The full table is in Appendix I.

When $N = 48$, the point number limit is 16. As $16 > 9$, so a positive correlation exists.

9.6 Care in using scatter diagrams

(1) Stratification is very important in using scatter diagrams.

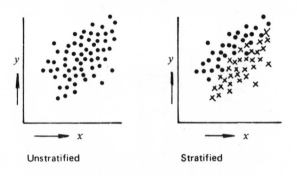

Unstratified   Stratified

Figure 9.6 Stratification in a scatter diagram

Figure 9.6 shows the relationship between raw material ingredient composition (x) and material strength (y). In the diagram on the left the data at hand were simply plotted, whereas the diagram on the right uses the same data – but the data were stratified (according to where the raw materials were bought) before plotting. This is an example of a situation where, on the whole, there seems to be no correlation but, when the data are stratified, a correlation is seen to exist. The reverse can also be true – when the data are stratified there seems to be no correlation but, when viewed as a whole, there really is. Therefore, when making cause-and-effect diagrams, stratification may be necessary before testing correlation; with scatter diagrams the plotting should be done in different colours or with different marks.

(2) Determining the range where correlation exists

Figure 9.7 is a scatter diagram that shows how product characteristic y was affected by altering production condition x. Even though we see the correlation during a stage in experimental tests, sometimes the correlation may not be observed under actual production conditions. Therefore, the apparent lack of correlation between x and y under actual production conditions should not be misread to theoretical conclusions that correlation does not exist under broader conditions.

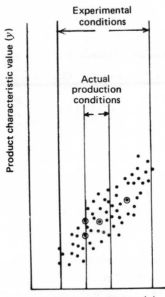

Figure 9.7 Correlation range limits

(3) Peaks and troughs on scatter diagrams

Under actual production conditions, peaks and troughs on scatter diagrams are very rare. But, when the points plot out as in figure 9.8, according to the above section on testing correlation with scatter diagrams, there should be no correlation. However, in this case the scatter diagram should be divided into two sections, by the line $A - A'$; the area to the left should be handled as a positive correlation while the area to the right is handled as a negative correlation. (The reverse applies to the diagram on the right side.)

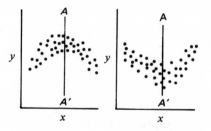

Figure 9.8 Scatter diagrams with peaks and troughs

We have studied much in this chapter, but if you can grasp the relationship between two things with a scatter diagram this alone will be of great use.

If you want to investigate the relationship between more than two causes, or causes and effects, there is also a double or multiple correlation analysis method. With the recent development of electronic computers to facilitate the calculations, the application of this method has become easier.

97

Chapter 10

Binomial probability paper

10.1 What is a binomial probability paper?

We have already studied data collection, histograms, cause-and-effect diagrams and control charts. I hope you are practising them actively. Now let us take a look at quality control activities.

When taking up a problem you must get an understanding of the actual situation. Pareto diagrams, histograms, graphs and control charts will be very useful in doing this. Next, find the causes of the problem through the use of a cause-and-effect diagram. Now you can analyze the data on the cause, or analyze the production process. To make this analysis smoothly, it will be necessary to use the proper statistical methods.

We therefore want to explain about a binomial probability paper which will enable you to easily test and estimate discrete values such as number of defectives and fraction defective, etc.

Statistical methods are thought to be difficult or bothersome, and consequently there is a tendency to avoid them on the job. However, using a simple chart, a binomial probability paper enables you to make tests or estimates of discrete values with almost no computing. It is precise and very practical for analyzing large amounts of data. Moreover, for continuous data expressed in plus, minus or order, a binomial probability paper can be used so that the testing and estimation of correlation can also be accomplished.

10.2 Structure of a binomial probability paper

A binomial probability paper is a graph that has a square root scale on both the vertical and horizontal axes. In other words, it is a form of square root paper calibrated in units of x at the distance $\sqrt{x}$. The technical terms are listed below and explained.

(1) Base: The base on a binomial probability paper is the distance from the origin, 0, to 1.

(2) Actual survey points: Any sample n could be divided into two charac-

teristics or actual survey values, say r (defectives) and $n - r$ (good products). These values, when plotted as points, may be denoted as ($n - r$, r) or (r, $n - r$). These points are called actual survey points. For example, if we find ten defective units in a sample of 100 units, the actual survey points of this sample would be (90, 10) or (10, 90). However, the number of accepted good units is normally put on the horizontal axis and should be expressed as (90, 10).

(3) Actual survey triangle: When the value of r is very small compared to the actual survey value $n - r$, there is in fact no stability with the actual survey point alone. In such a situation, a right-angled triangle is constructed for added safety, using ($n - r, r$), ($n - r, r + 1$) and ($n - r + 1$, r). This is called an actual survey triangle.

(4) Quarter circle: An arc which connects the horizontal and vertical axes at points (0, 100) and (100, 0) respectively is called a quarter circle.

(5) Split: A straight line which passes through the origin, 0, is called the split.

(6) Deviation: The length of a line from the actual survey point and perpendicular to the split is called the deviation.

(7) Short distance, medium distance, long distance: When the actual survey points are expressed as an actual survey triangle, the two lines from the apexes of the acute angles to the split are called the long and the short distance, depending on their length. The line from the centre of the oblique side of the actual survey triangle to the split is called the medium distance (see figure 10.1).

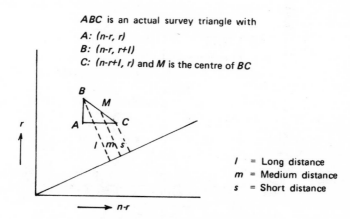

ABC is an actual survey triangle with

A: *(n-r, r)*

B: *(n-r, r+1)*

C: *(n-r+1, r)* and *M* is the centre of *BC*

l = Long distance
m = Medium distance
s = Short distance

Figure 10.1 Explanation of distances

(8) Range: When there are several actual survey points (p_1, q_1) and (p_2, q_2) . . . then the $\Sigma p_i : \Sigma q_i$ splits are drawn. The total distance between the furthest separated points on the upper and lower sides of the splits is called the range.

10.3 The test for population fraction defective

At a certain bottle manufacturing plant the fraction defective had been 15 per cent. Because the metal molds were old, they were repaired and 60 samples were taken from the first lot after the repair. There were six defectives. Can the fraction defective be said to have changed?

Step 1. Set up your hypothesis.

$$H_0 \ : \ p' \ = \ 0.15$$
$$H_1 \ : \ p' \ \neq \ 0.15$$

Step 2. Determine the level of significance or risk, alpha (α).

$$\alpha \ = \ 0.05$$

Step 3. Draw the split at 15 per cent as in figure 10.2 (for example, through the point dividing 85 accepted products from 15 defectives).

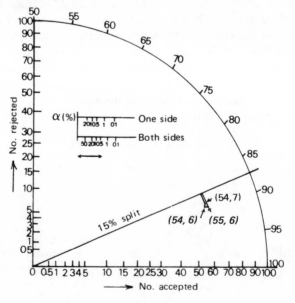

Figure 10.2

Step 4. Plot the actual survey points (54, 6), that is, the number accepted and the number rejected $(n - r, r)$, on the horizontal and vertical axes.

Step 5. Now construct the actual survey triangle (54, 6), (55, 6) and (54, 7), i.e., $(n - r, r)$, $(n - r + 1, r)$ and $(n - r, r + 1)$.

Step 6. Measure the distances on the perpendicular from the 15 per cent split to the furthest point of the actual survey triangle (55, 6) and the nearest point (54, 7).

Step 7. Comparing these distances with the α scale of 5 per cent to both sides of the split, we find that even the long distance is shorter than the length at 5 per cent of the α scale, so we know that this is a case of null hypothesis. In other words, it cannot be said that the fraction defective has changed.

Note 1: Whether the α scale is used on both sides of the split or only on one side depends upon the amount of information available beforehand. One side is used when the information is sufficient to indicate the trend; when the information is insufficient, both sides are used.

Note 2: In conducting an investigation by means of the α scale, when the hypothesis is rejected, that is, if the points are too scattered, compare the short distance against the distance on the α scale. But, when the hypothesis is accepted, use the long distance. The decision must be reserved, however, when the long distance has a 5 per cent risk or level of significance or when the short distance has no risk or significance. This often happens when the size of the sample is small. When the decision is thus reserved, it is necessary to take more samples or engage in detailed calculations.

10.4 Comparing two groups of paired corresponding data

The viscosity of an emulsion is one of its important characteristics. Because a wide dispersion in viscosity values of the emulsion being produced appeared recently, a cause-and-effect diagram was prepared, and it was assumed that there might be a discrepancy in the two lots being produced each day. Results obtained by processing data which had been accumulated in the past are shown in table 10.1. Is there a difference between the two lots?

---

*For α scale and R scale, refer to Appendix II.

Table 10.1

No	A	B		No	A	B	
1	35.7	24.6	+	21	23.5	32.4	−
2	39.0	26.8	+	22	40.0	22.4	+
3	49.7	31.1	+	23	33.6	34.8	−
4	45.5	26.8	+	24	47.5	31.3	+
5	40.0	26.4	+	25	29.0	40.1	−
6	25.4	24.5	+	26	39.2	24.6	+
7	25.3	37.9	−	27	35.1	49.7	−
8	37.9	33.5	+	28	42.9	32.5	+
9	25.7	22.9	+	29	26.0	40.2	−
10	44.6	31.3	+	30	49.4	32.9	+
11	30.2	35.7	−	31	42.7	38.8	+
12	40.2	26.8	+	32	32.6	33.5	−
13	24.6	38.2	−	33	44.4	40.6	+
14	20.0	30.2	−	34	38.8	31.6	+
15	20.2	29.0	−	35	33.0	31.8	+
16	31.3	28.8	+	36	44.5	20.6	+
17	23.5	25.7	−	37	31.9	27.2	+
18	39.2	28.6	+	38	38.0	21.8	+
19	31.3	30.0	+	39	23.4	39.1	−
20	41.3	27.9	+	40	35.2	26.7	+

Step 1. Compare the material in vats A and B. When the viscosity of the emulsion in A was greater than in B, this was indicated by a plus mark; a minus mark was used when it was lower than in B.

Step 2. Adding the plus and minus marks in the table, we find that there are 27 plus marks and 13 minus marks.

Step 3. Make an actual survey triangle on the binomial probability paper (using actual survey points 27 and 13), and compare the long distance and the short distance to the 50 per cent split with that of the α scale on both sides to the 50 per cent split. We find that both distances are longer than the distance from the 5 per cent α scale (that is, the triangle is outside the line representing the 5 per cent α scale). Thus there is risk or significance. We can now say that there is a difference between the emulsion from vat A and from vat B (see figure 10.3).

Note 1: In this example, where we are only concerned with differences in value and therefore only use plus and minus signs, we are applying what is called the sign test method. When A and B are equal, the zero sign is written. Usually, these zero values are excluded from further investigations. However, it will be safer to include them among the plus or minus values, whichever is smaller.

Note 2: As shown in figure 10.3, it is convenient to draw lines parallel to the split, on both sides at a distance of 1 per cent and 5 per cent, for the α scale. However, when using only one side of the split, it is sufficient to use one side of the α scale.

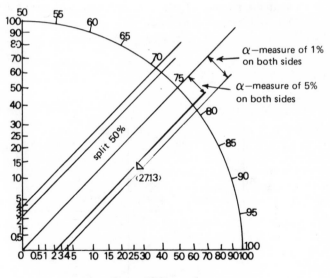

Figure 10.3

Note 3: Since there is no requirement that there be a normal distribution for the sign test, this method may also be applied to study the fraction defective and dispersion.

103

10.5 Test for correlation

(1) Using scatter diagrams

We assume that the softness of a certain cream is influenced by the purity of the wax in the cream. The company's inspection section has been asked to provide data for analysis and, after preparing a scatter diagram based on softness as measured at the stage of cream production, we have made figure 10.4. Can we say that there is a correlation between the purity of the wax and the softness of the cream? If there is a significant correlation, determine the correlation coefficient.

Step 1. Draw horizontal and vertical median lines on the scatter diagram so that there are equal numbers of points on the left and right sides, and equal numbers of points on the upper and lower parts.

Step 2. Label the four areas I, II, III and IV, as shown in figure 10.4. Count the number of points in each area. The results are: $n_1 = 27, n_2 = 13; n_3 = 27; n_4 = 13$.

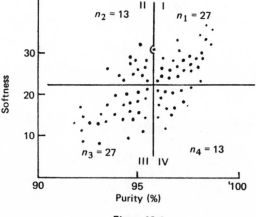

Figure 10.4

Step 3. Determine n_+ and n_-. The results are: $n_+ = n_1 + n_3 = 54; n_- = n_2 + n_4 = 26$.

Step 4. On a binomial probability paper, plot (n_+, n_-), that is (54, 26), and make an actual survey triangle. Compare the long and short distances with the distance from the 50 per cent split to the α scale on both sides. As a result, it is found that there is a significance, because the long and short distances are found to be beyond the 1 per cent α scale. We can conclude that there is a relationship between the purity of the wax and the softness of the cream (see figure 10.5).

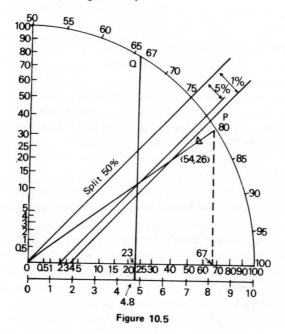

Figure 10.5

Step 5. Draw a split line from the origin and the actual survey point (54, 26) to the quarter circle. The point where it intercepts the quarter circle shall be marked *P*.

Step 6. Point *P* corresponds to the value of 67 on the horizontal axis. This same value, 67, on the radian scale of the quarter circle shall be called point *Q*.

105

Step 7. A vertical line is drawn from point Q, which intercepts the centimetre scale below the horizontal axis at the 4.8 centimetres point. This is calibrated ten times of the correlation coefficient r. Therefore $r = 0.48$, while the estimated value for the ratio of contribution is determined by the point at which the perpendicular intersects the horizontal axis; in this case it is 23 per cent.

Note: When testing for correlation by use of a binominal probability paper, for later convenience in determining the correlation coefficient, use the larger of $n_1 + n_3$ and $n_2 + n_4$ for the horizontal axis. If $n_1 + n_3$ is larger than $n_2 + n_4$, then the correlation is positive; if it is smaller, then the correlation is negative.

(2) Using graphs and control charts

In analyzing the production process, when two graphs have been made showing the paired data for two characteristics of the product, we can express these graphs statistically to determine the correlation. We can use two methods for this: one is based on the relation of points to a median line and the other uses the direction of the line connecting two consecutive points. The first method thus uses the absolute values of the data, and the second method is more detailed and free of any influence from the first.

For the first method, that is, determining correlation on the basis of whether points are above or below the median, the procedure is as follows. First, median lines are drawn on both graphs; plus signs are used to denote values above the medians while minus signs are used for those below the medians. When paired data have the same signs, this relationship is indicated by a plus sign. When paired data have different signs, this relationship is indicated by a minus sign. Then, these plus and minus signs are added up separately. Interpretation of the results is similar to that for a scatter diagram. When there are more plus signs than minus signs, there is a positive correlation. When there are more minus signs than plus signs, there is a negative correlation.

For the second method, concerning each of the two graphs, when the line joining one plotted point or data value to the next is ascending, this should be denoted by a plus sign; when the line is descending, this should be denoted by a minus sign. When there is no change in level, it should be shown by a zero. If the signs for paired lines are the same, this is indicated by a plus sign; if they differ, a minus sign is used. When zeros are involved, put in a '0'. The results are then studied in the same way as with the first method to determine the correlation. In this case, however, it is not necessary to draw a median line.

Note 1: The first method of determining the correlation resembles the use of scatter diagrams.

Note 2: In testing correlation by using graphs or control charts, this method is applicable even if the x and y axes do not represent a normal distribution. It can also be used for the investigation of causes of the fraction defective and dispersion. This method is also easy to use at the plant floor level.

Note 3: When investigating correlation by means of a binomial probability paper, the accuracy is impaired when there are relatively few points, so there should be at least 50 points or data values.

10.6 2 x 2 contingency tables

The results of this month's inspection of shipments of glass bottles received by companies A and B are shown in table 10.2. Is there a disparity in the acceptance ratios?

Table 10.2

	Accepted lots	Rejected lots	Total
Company A	86	2	88
Company B	44	8	52
Total	130	10	140

Step 1. Make actual survey triangles (86, 2) and (44, 8).

Step 2. Draw a 130:10 split.

Step 3. Determine the range. By comparison with the length of $N = 2$ of the R scale (5 per cent), we find that the distances are longer than the distance to the R scale. Therefore, there is a difference between the acceptance ratios of companies A and B (see figure 10.6).

107

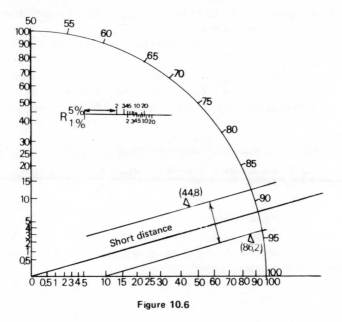

Figure 10.6

10.7 2 x m contingency tables

In connection with three new shades of lipstick (No. 501, No. 502 and No. 503) introduced this year, the data for the important characteristic of hardness have been plotted as in figure 10.7. Can it be said that the hardness is different depending on the lipstick shade?

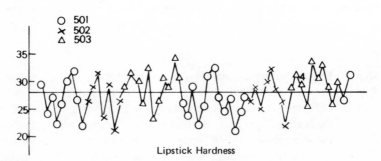

Lipstick Hardness

Figure 10.7

Step 1. Draw a horizontal line on the graph (figure 10.7), dividing the points into approximately equal numbers. Count the points for each product above and below it and prepare a 2 x 3 contingency table (table 10.3).

Table 10.3

	No 501	No 502	No 503	Total
Above	7	7	16	30
Below	17	8	5	30
Total	24	15	21	60

Step 2. Draw actual survey triangles on a binomial probability paper: for No. 501, (7, 17); for No. 502 (7, 8); for No. 503 (16, 5).

Step 3. Draw a 30:30 split.

Step 4. Determine the distance of the points furthest above and below the split. In this case, they are actual survey points for No. 501 (7, 18) above, and for No. 503 (17, 5) below.

Step 5. In comparing the length of this range with the $N = 3$ of the R scale (5 per cent), even the short distance is longer than R. Thus we can say that there is a difference in hardness depending on the lipstick shade (see figure 10.8).

Note 1: If it is difficult to use the binomial probability paper because the figures in the data are too large, divide the figures by 10 and use the $1/\sqrt{10}$ cm scale for testing. That means, measure the range of length obtained from the data multiplied by 1/10 with the cm scale, then obtain the actual length with the figures by utilizing the $1/\sqrt{10}$ scale drawn below.

Note 2: When testing with the above method, there is no need to construct the actual survey triangles. The actual survey values alone will be sufficient.

For the use of a binomial probability paper in statistical methods, the so-called simple method has been introduced above. In addition to this method, there are many other techniques that can be applied. However, this simple method alone is very helpful for a statistical determination of the fraction defective, the number of defectives and other problems, at the

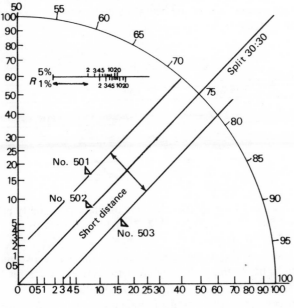

Figure 10.8

shop floor level. It is felt that the use of this simple method of using a binomial probability paper should be attempted before trying more advanced techniques at the actual production level. The above method should also produce a greater impact by stratifying data according to different machines, work teams, individual workers, raw materials, days or period of production or processing, and so on. It is therefore hoped that this method will be used fully since it can enable the users to gain a considerable amount of information about their work.

However, a word of caution: if the number of data is small, the differences will not be revealed clearly, and it will be dangerous to draw the conclusion that there is no significance. In such a case it is necessary either to obtain additional data or adopt a more precise method.

Chapter 11

Sampling

11.1 What is sampling?

In factories, many measures are taken on the basis of data. Before taking any action concerning quality control it is absolutely necessary to have data. For example, data are necessary to control temperature, pressure, speed and time in order to maintain the operating standards of equipment. Data are also necessary to control characteristic values of .materials and products, such as size, weight, intensity and substances. Finally, even efficiency, yield, fraction defective and cost can be termed data. These data indicate the situation of the process of a product, not the quality of the lot.

In most cases we get these data through sampling. Of course we cannot inspect every single product. So we take a sample and then we make an estimate for the entire lot According to Japan Industrial Standard Z 8101, "Glossary of Terms Used in Quality Control", the definition of the term "sample" is "that which is taken from a population for certain purposes".

Now, please look at figure 11.1. We take samples of finished *lots* of products in order to learn the nature of each entire lot, and we take samples from the *production line* to determine the conditions on the line, or to consider the future method of the process, and to obtain data for action. Thus, a group for which we plan to take action based upon a sample or data is called a *population*. In figure 11.1, (a) shows that, in the case of action on a production process, the population is considered to be a manufacturing process or work that occurs under fixed conditions. The products that come from that manufacturing process are considered to be infinite, so we call them an *infinite population*. This applies when the object of data is process control and analysis.

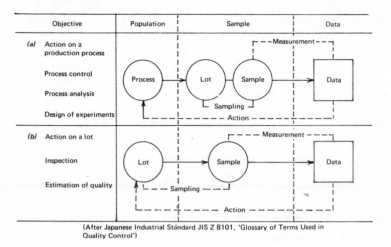

(After Japanese Industrial Standard JIS Z 8101, 'Glossary of Terms Used in Quality Control')

Figure 11.1 The relation between population, sample and data

Part of figure 11.1 (b) shows that, when it comes to action on a lot, the lot is always finite, such as 100 tons of charcoal or 50 dozen pencils. This is called a *finite population*. This is the object of inspection and evaluation of quality. Therefore, the purpose of collecting data from the samples taken in a given population is to gain proper knowledge of the population and thus to take suitable action.

11.2 Statistical thinking, and sampling

The data we collect are not all the same. They always contain dispersion — because there is an infinite number of causes of dispersion in the manufacturing process and even when production conditions are under a state of control, some dispersion cannot be avoided. There is dispersion between lots, between products in the same lot, and in some cases even in a single product.

Because of the dispersion that exists in lots or processes, they display *frequency distribution*. There are several ways of measuring this frequency distribution. But if the *mean value* (the value that determines the position of the frequency) and the amount showing dispersion (*variance* or *standard deviation*) can be found, then the feature of distribution can usually be determined.

Since populations display this frequency distribution, you must be careful to maintain a strictly *random sampling*. In other words, do not just select or pick up the good or bad pieces. Do not take samples from only one portion of the lot. The samples must be truly representative of the lot.

To evaluate a given lot, you have to estimate the frequency distribution of the lot, that is, the mean value and dispersion of the frequency distribution. However, for economic and technical reasons, it is hard for us to measure the entire lot, so we take samples from one part, measure them, and make our estimate of the mean value and dispersion of the lot. This means that when we discuss sampling we must consider economic, technical and statistical matters.

The conditions for sampling should be:
  1. correct
  2. reliable
  3. speedy
  4. economic

We must remember that the data values we get from our samples differ from those for the lot, and if there is any chance of confusing the two we should be careful and label them as shown in table 11.1.

Table 11.1 Population, samples and data

	Population	Sample
Mean value	Population mean μ	Sample mean $\bar{x}$
Variance	Population variance σ^2	Sample variance s^2
Standard deviation	Population standard deviation σ	Sample standard deviation s

11.3 Random sampling

(1) Conditions for random sampling

Most people think that a sample should be the best or the worst one in the group. However, since samples are collected to learn about the population, we must stop this kind of thinking. Random sampling is one way to overcome this.

Random sampling means that "we carry out sampling in such a way that every unit in a population will have an equal chance of being included in the sample with equal probability, regardless of the unit's appearance or position, that is, every part of the population must be exposed to the possibility of being taken as a sample". But, to take random samples from a population in this way is difficult and troublesome — and sometimes even impossible. For example, selecting random samples from a warehouse full of wrapped packages would be both difficult and expensive. Taking random samples for 100,000 tons of ore is impossible. Therefore, in such situations the samples are taken from conveyor belts or from the transferring lots during the manufacturing process.

(2) Random sampling method

a)   Simple random sampling

This method is simply to sample at random from a given population. It is used where there is no preliminary knowledge of things such as techniques or statistics. However, if the sampling is to be conducted by the manufacturer, it is better to make use of the preliminary knowledge for sampling, and therefore other sampling methods are preferable.

Example 1: Random sampling (the method for taking ten pieces out of 50 products based on a table of random numbers).

A table of random numbers has columns of numbers without order which appear with the same probability for 0 to 9.*

Step 1.   Choosing the page: Roll a dice and open to the page of the number which comes up (for a 6, page 6, etc).

Step 2.   Deciding where to start: Close your eyes and touch the table of random numbers with a pencil. Use the numbers in the two figures where the pencil struck. (If the numbers are 01 ∼ 50, there is no problem. Otherwise subtract 50 to bring them to 1 ∼ 50.) Next, in the same way decide the line. Assuming our pencil struck line 84; 50 from 84 is 34. So we start at line 34 and in the same way column 9.

Step 3.   In this case we have 50 products, so, from 1 to 100, we will select the first 10 which are in the 1 ∼ 50 range. Taking the numbers in page 2, line 34 from column 9, we have:

13,   20,   02,   44,   ~~95~~,   ~~94~~,   ~~64~~,   ~~85~~,   04,
05,   ~~72~~,   01,   32,   ~~90~~,   ~~75~~,   14,   ~~53~~,   ~~89~~,
~~74~~,   ~~60~~,   41,

In other words, you will have a random sampling if you take the following numbers of samples:

1, 2, 4, 5, 13, 14, 20, 32, 41, 44

*The random numbers referred to hereunder are from tables in accordance with JIS Z 9021 and copyrighted by the Nippon Kagaku Gijutsu Remmei, 10-11 Sendagaya 5-chome, Shibuya-ku, Tokyo.

When using dice, follow this procedure: Usually hexagonal dice numbered from 1 to 6 are used to obtain random numbers up to 6. A 20-faced dice has room for each number from 0 to 9 to be written twice. If you roll it once, you can get one figure of random numbers; if you roll it twice or have a pair of different coloured dice, you can get two figures. This is convenient for use on the job.

b) Random number generating device

There are various types which adopt this method. The drawing or lottery type, the turret type and the windmill type are some examples.

Example 2: Systematic sampling. Simple random sampling from a population is often difficult. In such situations, one should sample at fixed intervals. This is called *systematic sampling*. The method for conducting systematic sampling is as follows. Let us suppose that we are going to take 5 samples out of 150 products. We number the products and take samples at fixed intervals. The sampling ratio is 1/30, so we take a number from $1 \sim 30$ from the table of random numbers. If we happen to select 05, we add 30, and then 60 (2 x 30), and so on, as follows:

$$05, \; 5 + 30 = 35, \; 65, \; 95, \; 125$$

We should then take the products that have these numbers as samples.

11.4 Sampling error

If we examined the entire lot after sampling and found our sample values were somewhat different from the lot values then we would say there was error. This error can be divided into two categories: bias and dispersion.

(1) Bias

The result of taking only the best ones for samples or taking samples with only a certain value will be that the *sample mean* differs from the *population mean*. This is called bias (see figure 11.2). Typical causes of bias are:

1. Taking only the biggest pieces of iron ore
2. Taking only from one edge of a long layer
3. Sampling in only the first stage of smelting
4. Sampling only the surface of liquid at rest

The sample mean $\bar{x}$ will turn out as in figure 11.2(a) if you use sampling methods such as these. So this must be avoided.

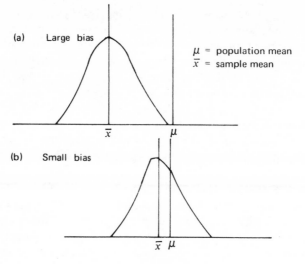

Figure 11.2 Bias

(2) Dispersion (precision)

The value of samples taken repeatedly from one lot is put into a histogram. The standard deviation (s) of the histogram shows the degree of precision.

We often hear the expression "error of plus or minus one per cent". But this expression shows a lack of statistical knowledge. Precision must be specified in numerical values, such as standard deviation is, for instance σ of 0.5%, $\bar{R}$ of r = 2 is 0.4%. It is necessary to experiment to find sampling precision.

(3) Sampling error

Uncontrolled bias, dispersion or both and uncontrolled samples will cause what is called error. However, the word "error" is ambiguous and does not specify whether it means bias or precision or reliability. To achieve reliability, that is to maintain control over the sampling processes, the following things are necessary:

1. An analysis of the causes of bias and how to ensure precision
2. Issuing instructions for controlling these causes
3. Making certain the instructions are followed (through worker education and training)
4. Control of the measuring instruments and equipment

11.5 Types of sampling

(1) Random sampling

This means taking samples at random from the entire lot. See above and figure 11.3.

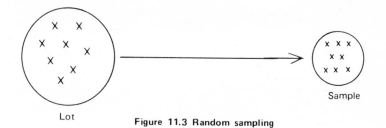

Figure 11.3 Random sampling

(2) Two-stage sampling

In the first stage, take primary units from a lot. Next, in the second stage, take secondary samples from the sampled primary units. This method is commonly used in factories (see figure 11.4).

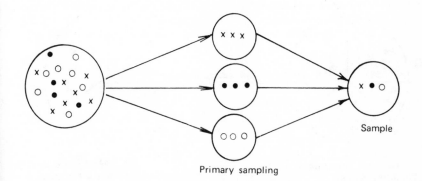

Figure 11.4 Two-stage sampling

117

(3) Stratified sampling

The lot is divided into several strata and samples are taken from each. However, the samples from each strata are taken at random. The closer the strata homogeneity, the more precise the overall samples will be (see figure 11.5).

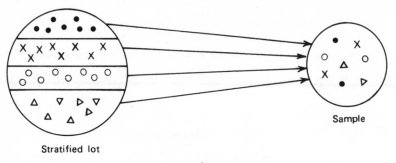

Figure 11.5 Stratified sampling

(4) Cluster sampling

In factories where products are the object of sampling, this method (see 11.6) is not used very often. If the clustering is not done properly, precision will be poor or bias will appear. To make good clusters, all parts of the lots must be represented in the cluster in equal proportion.

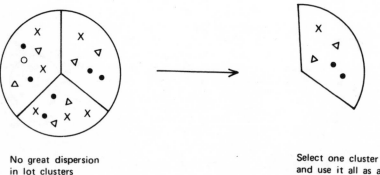

Figure 11.6 Cluster sampling

(5) Selected sampling

To find the mean value of the whole lot, rather than take a representative sampling of the whole lot, a sample can be taken from only one special part and, on the basis of that value, the lot value is estimated. This is very commonly used in process control for manufacturing. For example, the following methods can be used for obtaining selected samples (see figure 11.6):

1. Taking sample threads, films or coils from one edge of a long belt
2. Sampling at a specific time
3. Sampling only the ore out of a mixture of ore and sand

Selected samples are more precise than simple random samples and the method is easy and economical, but there is always some bias from the population mean.

Chapter 12

Sampling inspection

12.1 What is sampling inspection?

When we go out to buy something, we take a look at a number of articles and examine the quality before we decide whether to buy it or not. Let us think about this for a moment. When judging these articles we have selected, we are actually examining samples, and we may end up buying the article only if all the samples are of good quality. On the other hand, when it really comes to the stage of making a decision, we may compromise and buy the article even if there are a few defectives in the samples. This can be called a sampling inspection. But the sampling inspection we are going to discuss now differs greatly. This difference is important, so please bear it in mind. It may seem that picking up a number of samples from a large quantity of articles and then examining them to decide whether the lot is acceptable or not is the same sampling inspection method that has been practised for a long time. However, there is a big difference. We must consider the number of defectives there may be in a box and the fraction defective we will consider acceptable; then, after determining the adequate number of samples to be taken and the level of acceptance or rejection, the sampling inspection is carried out. It is thus conducted on a statistical basis. This is fundamental. The following sampling inspections are carried out according to this concept.

12.2 Problems of total inspection

On the whole, complete quality inspection of each and every product (called "total inspection") is impossible. But it is necessary to thoroughly inspect quality characteristics which, because they are unstable, result in defects, as well as vital points that affect product life which may be inspected at reasonable cost. Do not be misled into carrying out inadequate total inspection on too many quality characteristics (that is, on many different inspection items) and then delivering or receiving products on that basis. This will result in complaints both within the company and outside.

When the number of inspectors is limited, increasing the number of items to be inspected by even one means that the time available for inspecting each characteristic will have to be shortened, or some other important inspection item will have to be dropped.*

To avoid the problems involved in total inspection, as outlined above, it is necessary to determine just how many characteristics will be inspected and which inspection method to use. Moreover, the target for the quality guarantee of accepted products must be set at 100 per cent, and controlled so that it is achieved. Remember that even after repeating total inspections time after time, all of us are liable to miss items occasionally. Knowledge of sampling inspection (in terms of inspection cost and quality assurance) is necessary for rational inspection.

12.3 Situations where sampling inspection is necessary

1. Destructive testing: a situation where inspection is not possible without destroying the article chemically or physically.
2. Inspecting long lengths of goods: copper coil, photographic film, paper, textiles, thread, etc are all difficult to unroll for inspection.
3. Inspecting large amounts: nuts, screws, bolts, etc are products made in large quantities and at high speed.

Sampling inspections are also applied often in the following situations:

4. When lower inspection costs are desired.
5. When it is desired to stimulate the maker and/or the buyer.
6. When there are many items or areas to be inspected.

12.4 Lot quality

We have a lot of 1,000 ($N = 1,000$), and a fraction defective of 5 per cent ($p = 5\%$). If we inspect ten samples ($n = 10$), what will the result be?

We put 1,000 steel balls in the box as shown in figure 12.1 and then mix them. The number of defective balls for the lot is 50, and they are painted red. We take ten balls out at random. We put the ten back in and

---

*In Japan, most of the companies apply the self-inspection system. The self-inspection system means that most of the quality characteristics are inspected by factory workers, not inspectors. So in Japan the percentage of inspectors to workers is only 1 to 5 per cent.

take out ten again, and so on, until we've repeated this 100 times. Table 2.1 shows the results. Although there are 50 balls painted red among the 1,000, when taking $n = 10$ out at a time and repeating this, we did not get a red ball in 59 tries out of 100. If a lot were to be judged unacceptable when one red ball was found among ten, then 59 times out of the 100 lot would be regarded as acceptable.

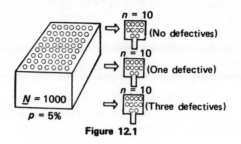

Figure 12.1

Table 12. 1

Number of defective products	Number of times appearing
0	59
1	32
2	8
3	1

Now, let's increase the size of our sample to 30 ($n = 30$). Using the same method we ended up with the results shown in table 12.2 and figure 12.2. In other words, even with $p = 5\%$, the lot is accepted 21 times out

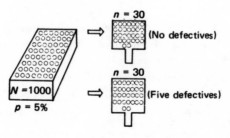

Figure 12.2

Table 12.2

Number of defective products	Number of times appearing
0	21
1	34
2	27
3	13
4	4
5	1

of 100. Continuing this experiment we increase our sample size to 100 ($n = 100$). The results are shown in table 12.3.

Table 12.3

Number of defects	Number of times appearing
0	—
1	3
2	8
3	14
4	18
5	19
6	16
7	11
8	6
9	4
10	1

Now we see that when $N = 1,000$, $p = 5\%$, and the size of our sample is

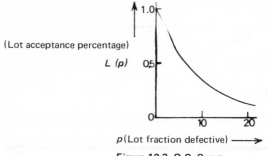

(Lot acceptance percentage)

L (p)

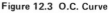

p(Lot fraction defective) ——→

Figure 12.3 O.C. Curve

$n = 100$, there is almost no chance of the lot being accepted on the basis of inspections in which no red ball was found.

We also see that the most red balls (defectives) which we came up with was five in the case of sample size $n = 100$. This shows that we can estimate the lot's fraction defective to be 5 per cent.

As you have seen, the number of times defectives appear depends on the size of the sample. With $n = 10$, the sampling inspection is meaningless. Sampling inspections must be conducted with this principle in mind. In other words, you must be aware of what is called the *operating characteristic curve*. As you see in figure 12.3, when $N = 1,000$, $n = 10$, and the acceptance number $c = 0$, the rate at which the lot is accepted will differ in accordance with p (fraction defective). This can be proven in experiment.

12.5 OC (operating characteristics) curves and acceptance sampling

If we inspect with values of $n = 100$ (size of sample) and $c = 2$ (allowable number of defectives), what will the acceptance percentage (or probability of acceptance) of a lot with 2 per cent defectives be? Assuming that the lot consists of over 1,000 pieces and the fraction defective is small, the probability of acceptance can be determined by using the Poisson distribution. The lot will be accepted if the number of defectives in randomly chosen samples is zero, one, or two.

The probability of acceptance will be as follows:

Probability of acceptance	=	percentage of times with no defective in samples	+	percentage of times with one defective in samples	+	percentage of times with two defectives in samples

In this manner, sample inspection conducted under the condition of $n = 100$, $c = 2$ revealed that the probability of acceptance of a lot with 2 per cent defectives is 0.68 (accepted 68 times out of 100). An operating characteristics curve, or characteristics curve of sample inspection or characteristic inspection curve, is a graph which shows the probability of acceptance of lots with fraction defective running from 0 per cent to 100 per cent. The lot per cent defective is shown on the horizontal axis and the lot acceptance probability is shown on the vertical axis (see figure 12.4).

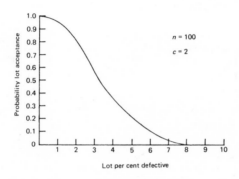

Figure 12.4

Let us consider the meaning of the OC curve. Here are some abbreviations which have been taken from JIS Z 9002:

p_0 : the upper limit for the acceptable fraction defective in a lot.

p_1 : the lower limit for rejectable fraction defective in a lot.

α : producer's risk (the percentage that a lot with p_0 fraction defective would be rejected).

β : consumer's risk (the percentage that a lot with p_1 fraction defective would be accepted).

p_0 is the fraction defective in a lot produced with the present equipment, workers, materials and methods, and which the producer requests the consumers to accept and the consumers, for their part, find reasonable.

p_1 is the fraction defective in a lot that the consumers would want to reject as being of bad quality and which the producer would not wish to distribute.

However, in sampling inspections acceptable lots are sometimes rejected while lots which are bad are sometimes accepted. The former situation is called producer's risk (written: α) and the latter situation is called consumer's risk (written: β). Generally, $\alpha = 0.05$ and $\beta = 0.10$.

Figure 12.5 shows the OC curve for:

$N = 1,000$ (lot size)
$n = 10$ (sample size)
$c = 0$ (allowable number of defectives)
$p_0 = 0.512\%$ (upper limit of acceptable fraction defective)
$p_1 = 20.6\%$ (lower limit of rejectable fraction defective)
$\alpha = 0.05$ (producer's risk)
$\beta = 0.10$ (consumer's risk)

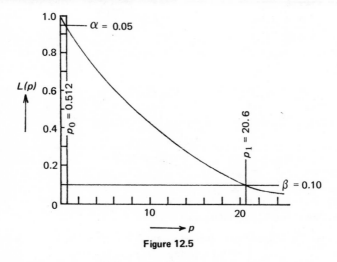

Figure 12.5

As can be seen from the above, when making sampling inspections it is necessary to consider p_0 and p_1 and also to determine n and c. This calls for some complicated computing, so generally a sampling inspection table such as table 12.4 is used.

(1) Standard single sampling inspection by attributes in case of defectives (JIS Z 9002)

Sampling inspections based on operating characteristics curves are not designed to even include the action of selecting the lots to be rejected, because this type of inspection is meant to determine whether a lot is acceptable or not.

Table 12.4 Table of standard single sampling inspection by attributes ($\alpha = 0.05$, $\beta = 0.10$)

Small type = n, bold type = c

p_0 (%) \\ p_1 (%)	0.71–0.90	0.91–1.12	1.13–1.40	1.41–1.80	1.81–2.24	2.25–2.80	2.81–3.55	3.56–4.50	4.51–5.60	5.61–7.10	7.11–9.00	9.01–11.2	11.3–14.0	14.1–18.0	18.1–22.4	22.5–28.0	28.1–35.5
0.090–0.112	*	400 **1**	→	↓	→	↑	→	50 **0**	→	→	→	↓	→	→	→	→	→
0.113–0.140	*	↓	300 **1**	→	↓	→	→	↓	→	40 **0**	→	→	↓	→	→	→	→
0.141–0.180	*	500 **2**	→	250 **1**	→	↓	→	→	↓	→	30 **0**	→	→	↓	→	→	→
0.181–0.224	*	↓	400 **2**	→	200 **1**	→	↓	→	→	↓	→	20 **0**	→	→	↓	→	→
0.225–0.280	*	↓	500 **3**	300 **2**	→	150 **1**	→	↓	→	→	↓	→	20 **0**	→	→	↓	→
0.281–0.355	*	↓	↓	400 **3**	250 **2**	→	100 **1**	→	↓	→	→	↓	→	15 **0**	→	→	↓
0.356–0.450	*	*	↓	500 **4**	300 **3**	200 **2**	→	100 **1**	→	↓	→	→	↓	→	15 **0**	→	→
0.451–0.560	*	*	↓	↓	400 **4**	250 **3**	150 **2**	80 **1**	→	↓	→	→	→	↓	10 **0**	→	→
0.561–0.710	*	*	*	↓	500 **6**	300 **4**	200 **3**	120 **2**	60 **1**	→	↓	→	→	→	↓	7 **0**	→
0.711–0.900	*	*	*	↓	*	400 **6**	250 **4**	150 **3**	100 **2**	50 **1**	→	↓	→	→	→	↓	5 **0**
0.901–1.12	*	*	*	*	*	500 **6**	300 **6**	200 **4**	120 **3**	80 **2**	40 **1**	→	↓	→	→	→	↓
1.13–1.40			*	*	*	*	250 **6**	200 **4**	150 **4**	100 **3**	60 **2**	30 **1**	→	↓	→	→	→
1.41–1.80				*	*	*	*	150 **6**	120 **4**	80 **3**	50 **2**	25 **1**	20 **1**	→	↓	→	→
1.81–2.24					*	*	*	100 **6**	100 **4**	60 **3**	40 **2**	20 **1**	15 **1**	→	↓	→	→
2.25–2.80						*	*	*	60 **4**	50 **3**	30 **2**	20 **1**	15 **1**	→	↓	→	→
2.81–3.55							*	*	50 **4**	40 **3**	25 **2**	15 **1**	→	↓	→	→	→
3.56–4.50								*	40 **4**	30 **3**	20 **2**	15 **1**	→	→	→	→	→
4.51–5.60									30 **4**	25 **3**	15 **2**	10 **1**	→	→	→	→	→
5.61–7.10										20 **4**	15 **2**	10 **1**	→	→	→	→	→
7.11–9.00											15 **3**	10 **2**	→	→	→	→	→
9.01–11.2												10 **3**	→	→	→	→	→

Use the first column of n, c in the direction of the arrow. There are no sampling methods for the blank columns.

Example: For rivet making, suppose we want to accept lots whose fraction defective was $p_0 = 2\%$ on the basis of inspection of the rivet diameter. Those where $p_1 = 12\%$, we wish to reject. How should we determine the number of samples to be taken(n) and the allowable number of defectives (c) using standard single sampling inspection (JIS Z 9002)?

Remarks: Using table 12.4, we find from the column where $p_0 = 2\%$ and $p_1 = 12\%$ intersect, that the value of $n = 40$ and $c = 2$.

However, there is one thing we have to consider. With the value given for p_0 and p_1, the table will give us sample size and acceptance number without regard to lot size. Keep the following points in mind:

a   Where the production process is in a controlled state: if the process is well controlled, try to keep the lots large as this will decrease the total number of inspections.

b   Where the production process is not in a controlled state: if it is in a very unstable state, it is better to keep the lots small.

c   Where there is little information about the production process: first inspect with the lots small and, as information accumulates, increase the lot size.

Points to keep in mind when determining p_0 and p_1:

P_0 and p_1 are generally fixed through agreement between the producers and the consumers. However, it is important to fix p_0 and p_1 values taking into consideration the loss caused by rejection of good lots or acceptance of bad lots which are related to quality guarantees level, inspection expenses and the size of lots. If $p_0 = p_1$, then total inspection must be undertaken. Therefore, it is generally recommended that $p_1/p_0 = 4 \sim 10$.

(2) American Military Standard (MIL-STD-105D)

The American Military Standard was developed so that economical inspections of goods procured by the military could be assured. It was first put into use in August 1950 and since then has undergone many revisions, from MIL-STD-105A (September, 1950) to MIL-STD-105D (April, 1963), which is the current designation. Today many sampling inspections use MIL-STD-105D, but some people hesitate to use it. There is not enough space to go deeper into that problem here, but the essentials are as follows:

a   The standard favours the consumer.

b   The procedures for adjusting the severity of the inspection are too complicated and unwieldy.

c   The conditions for changing to a reduced inspection are sometimes strict.

d   The consumer's risk with a reduced inspection is very great.

These problems will probably result in further revision of MIL-STD-105D. This MIL-STD-105D is an adjusted sampling inspection; its characteristic is that the severity of the inspection is adjusted according to the quality of the products presented for inspection and to stimuli to apply the total quality control system to the vendor. For this purpose the quality limit is set according to the Acceptable Quality Level (AQL).

This AQL is the upper limit of the per cent defective that is acceptable as being satisfactory in terms of the production process average. Severity of inspection is rated as normal, reduced or tightened, and expressed on an OC curve as shown in figure 12.6 and table 12.5. There are usually three levels for inspection, but in special cases there may be four. These levels bear no relation to severity. The lower the inspection level, the smaller the sample size, and the lower the inspection cost. However, as the producer's

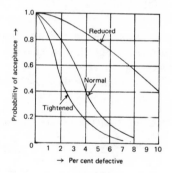

Figure 12.6

AQL=1%   **Table 12.5**

	n	A_c	R_e
Reduced inspection	32	1 (2)	3
Normal inspection	80	2	3
Tightened inspection	80	1	2

n = Number of samples

A_c = Acceptance number

R_e = Rejection number

risk and consumer's risk increase, the following rules should be applied:

Inspection level I: when the inspection cost is comparatively high.
Inspection level II: ordinary cases.
Inspection level III: when inspection costs are low
Inspection level S-1 to S-4: when the cost of destructive testing is high.

Inspection procedure

Step 1. Determine the quality level (set the actual inspection standards).
Step 2. Establish the AQL.
Step 3. Determine the inspection level.
Step 4. Determine the sampling inspection method or plan.
Step 5. Determine the severity of the inspection.
Step 6. Determine the composition and size of the lot to be inspected.
Step 7. Determine the severity of the sampling inspection method or plan (use appropriate tables for this).
Step 8. Draw sample items.
Step 9. Inspect each sample item.
Step 10. Determine whether to accept or reject the inspection lot.
Step 11. Take post-inspection action on the lot (return rejected items, conduct 100 per cent inspection to eliminate defectives, repair rejected items etc).
Step 12. Record the inspection results (as they will be needed for adjusting the severity of future inspections).

Table 12.6 MIL Table I Sample size code letters

Lot size		Special inspection levels				Normal inspection levels		
		S-1	S-2	S-3	S-4	I	II	III
2-	8	A	A	A	A	A	A	B
9-	15	A	A	A	A	A	B	C
16-	25	A	A	B	B	B	C	D
26-	50	A	B	B	C	C	D	E
51-	90	B	B	C	C	C	E	F
91-	150	B	B	C	D	D	F	G
151-	280	B	C	D	E	E	G	H
281-	500	B	C	D	E	F	H	J
501-	1,200	C	C	E	F	G	J	K
1,201-	3,200	C	D	E	G	H	K	L
3,201-	10,000	C	D	F	G	J	L	M
10,001-	35,000	C	D	F	H	K	M	N
35,001-	150,000	D	E	G	J	L	N	P
150,001-	500,000	D	E	G	J	M	P	Q
Over	500,000	L	E	H	K	N	Q	R

Table 12.7 MIL Table II-A Master table for normal inspection (single sampling)

Each cell shows the Acceptance number (Ac) and Rejection number (Re). AQLs listed are for normal inspection.

Sample size code letter	Sample size (n)	0.010	0.015	0.025	0.040	0.065	0.10	0.15	0.25	0.40	0.65	1.0	1.5	2.5	4.0	6.5	10	15	25	40	65	100	150	250	400	650	1000
A	2																↓	0 1	1 2	2 3	3 4	5 6	7 8	10 11	14 15	21 22	30 31
B	3															↓	0 1	1 2	2 3	3 4	5 6	7 8	10 11	14 15	21 22	30 31	44 45
C	5														↓	0 1	1 2	2 3	3 4	5 6	7 8	10 11	14 15	21 22	30 31	44 45	↑
D	8													↓	0 1	1 2	2 3	3 4	5 6	7 8	10 11	14 15	21 22	30 31	44 45	↑	
E	13												↓	0 1	1 2	2 3	3 4	5 6	7 8	10 11	14 15	21 22	30 31	44 45	↑		
F	20											↓	0 1	1 2	2 3	3 4	5 6	7 8	10 11	14 15	21 22	30 31	44 45	↑			
G	32										↓	0 1	1 2	2 3	3 4	5 6	7 8	10 11	14 15	21 22	30 31	44 45	↑				
H	50									↓	0 1	1 2	2 3	3 4	5 6	7 8	10 11	14 15	21 22	30 31	44 45	↑					
J	80								↓	0 1	1 2	2 3	3 4	5 6	7 8	10 11	14 15	21 22	30 31	44 45	↑						
K	125							↓	0 1	1 2	2 3	3 4	5 6	7 8	10 11	14 15	21 22	30 31	44 45	↑							
L	200						↓	0 1	1 2	2 3	3 4	5 6	7 8	10 11	14 15	21 22	30 31	44 45	↑								
M	315					↓	0 1	1 2	2 3	3 4	5 6	7 8	10 11	14 15	21 22	30 31	44 45	↑									
N	500				↓	0 1	1 2	2 3	3 4	5 6	7 8	10 11	14 15	21 22	30 31	44 45	↑										
P	800			↓	0 1	1 2	2 3	3 4	5 6	7 8	10 11	14 15	21 22	30 31	44 45	↑											
Q	1250		↓	0 1	1 2	2 3	3 4	5 6	7 8	10 11	14 15	21 22	30 31	44 45	↑												
R	2000	↓	0 1	1 2	2 3	3 4	5 6	7 8	10 11	14 15	21 22	30 31	44 45	↑													

↓ = Use first sampling plan below arrow. When sample size equals or exceeds lot size, do total (100 per cent) inspection.

↑ = Use first sampling plan above arrow.

Ac = Acceptance number

Re = Rejection number

Table 12.8 MIL Table II-B Master table for tightened inspection (single sampling)

AQLs (tightened inspection). Each AQL cell below shows "Ac Re" (Ac = Acceptance number, Re = Rejection number); ↓ and ↑ denote arrows.

Code	n	0.010	0.015	0.025	0.040	0.065	0.10	0.15	0.25	0.40	0.65	1.0	1.5	2.5	4.0	6.5	10	15	25	40	65	100	150	250	400	650	1000
A	2	↓	↓	↓	↓	↓	↓	↓	↓	↓	↓	↓	↓	↓	↓	↓	↓	↓	0 1	1 2	2 3	3 4	5 6	8 9	12 13	18 19	27 28
B	3	↓	↓	↓	↓	↓	↓	↓	↓	↓	↓	↓	↓	↓	↓	↓	↓	0 1	1 2	2 3	3 4	5 6	8 9	12 13	18 19	27 28	41 42
C	5	↓	↓	↓	↓	↓	↓	↓	↓	↓	↓	↓	↓	↓	↓	↓	0 1	1 2	2 3	3 4	5 6	8 9	12 13	18 19	27 28	41 42	↑
D	8	↓	↓	↓	↓	↓	↓	↓	↓	↓	↓	↓	↓	↓	↓	0 1	1 2	2 3	3 4	5 6	8 9	12 13	18 19	27 28	41 42	↑	↑
E	13	↓	↓	↓	↓	↓	↓	↓	↓	↓	↓	↓	↓	↓	0 1	1 2	2 3	3 4	5 6	8 9	12 13	18 19	27 28	41 42	↑	↑	↑
F	20	↓	↓	↓	↓	↓	↓	↓	↓	↓	↓	↓	↓	0 1	1 2	2 3	3 4	5 6	8 9	12 13	18 19	27 28	41 42	↑	↑	↑	↑
G	32	↓	↓	↓	↓	↓	↓	↓	↓	↓	↓	↓	0 1	1 2	2 3	3 4	5 6	8 9	12 13	18 19	27 28	41 42	↑	↑	↑	↑	↑
H	50	↓	↓	↓	↓	↓	↓	↓	↓	↓	↓	0 1	1 2	2 3	3 4	5 6	8 9	12 13	18 19	27 28	41 42	↑	↑	↑	↑	↑	↑
J	80	↓	↓	↓	↓	↓	↓	↓	↓	↓	0 1	1 2	2 3	3 4	5 6	8 9	12 13	18 19	27 28	41 42	↑	↑	↑	↑	↑	↑	↑
K	125	↓	↓	↓	↓	↓	↓	↓	↓	0 1	1 2	2 3	3 4	5 6	8 9	12 13	18 19	27 28	41 42	↑	↑	↑	↑	↑	↑	↑	↑
L	200	↓	↓	↓	↓	↓	↓	↓	0 1	1 2	2 3	3 4	5 6	8 9	12 13	18 19	27 28	41 42	↑	↑	↑	↑	↑	↑	↑	↑	↑
M	315	↓	↓	↓	↓	↓	↓	0 1	1 2	2 3	3 4	5 6	8 9	12 13	18 19	27 28	41 42	↑	↑	↑	↑	↑	↑	↑	↑	↑	↑
N	500	↓	↓	↓	↓	↓	0 1	1 2	2 3	3 4	5 6	8 9	12 13	18 19	27 28	41 42	↑	↑	↑	↑	↑	↑	↑	↑	↑	↑	↑
P	800	↓	↓	↓	↓	0 1	1 2	2 3	3 4	5 6	8 9	12 13	18 19	27 28	41 42	↑	↑	↑	↑	↑	↑	↑	↑	↑	↑	↑	↑
Q	1250	↓	↓	↓	0 1	1 2	2 3	3 4	5 6	8 9	12 13	18 19	27 28	41 42	↑	↑	↑	↑	↑	↑	↑	↑	↑	↑	↑	↑	↑
R	2000	↓	↓	0 1	1 2	2 3	3 4	5 6	8 9	12 13	18 19	27 28	41 42	↑	↑	↑	↑	↑	↑	↑	↑	↑	↑	↑	↑	↑	↑
S	3150	↓	0 1	1 2	2 3	3 4	5 6	8 9	12 13	18 19	27 28	41 42	↑	↑	↑	↑	↑	↑	↑	↑	↑	↑	↑	↑	↑	↑	↑

↓ = Use first sampling plan below arrow. When sample size equals or exceeds lot size, do 100 per cent inspection.

↑ = Use first sampling plan above arrow.

Ac = Acceptance number

Re = Rejection number

Table 12.9 MIL Table II-C Master table for reduced inspection (single sampling)

AQLs (reduced inspection)†

Legend: each AQL cell shows **Ac** (acceptance number) / **Re** (rejection number). ↓ = use first sampling plan below arrow. ↑ = use first sampling plan above arrow.

Code	n	0.010	0.015	0.025	0.040	0.065	0.10	0.15	0.25	0.40	0.65	1.0	1.5	2.5	4.0	6.5	10	15	25	40	65	100	150	250	400	650	1000
A	2	↓	↓	↓	↓	↓	↓	↓	↓	↓	↓	↓	↓	↓	↓	0 1	0 2	1 3	1 4	2 5	3 6	5 8	7 10	10 13	14 17	21 24	30 31
B	2	↓	↓	↓	↓	↓	↓	↓	↓	↓	↓	↓	↓	↓	↓	0 1	0 2	1 3	1 4	2 5	3 6	5 8	7 10	10 13	14 17	21 24	30 31
C	2	↓	↓	↓	↓	↓	↓	↓	↓	↓	↓	↓	↓	↓	↓	0 1	0 2	1 3	1 4	2 5	3 6	5 8	7 10	10 13	14 17	21 24	30 31
D	3	↓	↓	↓	↓	↓	↓	↓	↓	↓	↓	↓	↓	↓	0 1	0 2	1 3	1 4	2 5	3 6	5 8	7 10	10 13	14 17	21 24	30 31	↑
E	5	↓	↓	↓	↓	↓	↓	↓	↓	↓	↓	↓	↓	0 1	0 2	1 3	1 4	2 5	3 6	5 8	7 10	10 13	14 17	21 24	30 31	↑	↑
F	8	↓	↓	↓	↓	↓	↓	↓	↓	↓	↓	↓	0 1	0 2	1 3	1 4	2 5	3 6	5 8	7 10	10 13	14 17	21 24	30 31	↑	↑	↑
G	13	↓	↓	↓	↓	↓	↓	↓	↓	↓	↓	0 1	0 2	1 3	1 4	2 5	3 6	5 8	7 10	10 13	14 17	21 24	30 31	↑	↑	↑	↑
H	20	↓	↓	↓	↓	↓	↓	↓	↓	↓	0 1	0 2	1 3	1 4	2 5	3 6	5 8	7 10	10 13	14 17	21 24	30 31	↑	↑	↑	↑	↑
J	32	↓	↓	↓	↓	↓	↓	↓	↓	0 1	0 2	1 3	1 4	2 5	3 6	5 8	7 10	10 13	14 17	21 24	30 31	↑	↑	↑	↑	↑	↑
K	50	↓	↓	↓	↓	↓	↓	↓	0 1	0 2	1 3	1 4	2 5	3 6	5 8	7 10	10 13	14 17	21 24	30 31	↑	↑	↑	↑	↑	↑	↑
L	80	↓	↓	↓	↓	↓	↓	0 1	0 2	1 3	1 4	2 5	3 6	5 8	7 10	10 13	14 17	21 24	30 31	↑	↑	↑	↑	↑	↑	↑	↑
M	125	↓	↓	↓	↓	↓	0 1	0 2	1 3	1 4	2 5	3 6	5 8	7 10	10 13	14 17	21 24	30 31	↑	↑	↑	↑	↑	↑	↑	↑	↑
N	200	↓	↓	↓	↓	0 1	0 2	1 3	1 4	2 5	3 6	5 8	7 10	10 13	14 17	21 24	30 31	↑	↑	↑	↑	↑	↑	↑	↑	↑	↑
P	315	↓	↓	↓	0 1	0 2	1 3	1 4	2 5	3 6	5 8	7 10	10 13	14 17	21 24	30 31	↑	↑	↑	↑	↑	↑	↑	↑	↑	↑	↑
Q	500	↓	↓	0 1	0 2	1 3	1 4	2 5	3 6	5 8	7 10	10 13	14 17	21 24	30 31	↑	↑	↑	↑	↑	↑	↑	↑	↑	↑	↑	↑
R	800	↓	0 1	0 2	1 3	1 4	2 5	3 6	5 8	7 10	10 13	14 17	21 24	30 31	↑	↑	↑	↑	↑	↑	↑	↑	↑	↑	↑	↑	↑

↓ = Use first sampling plan below arrow. When sample size equals or exceeds lot size, do 100 per cent inspection.

↑ = Use first sampling plan above arrow.

Ac = Acceptance number

Re = Rejection number

† If the figure exceeds the acceptance number but is below rejection number, this lot is passed, but switch to normal inspection for the next lot.

133

Table 12.10 MIL Table VIII Limits for reduced inspection

Number of sample units in latest 10 lots	AQLs																									
	0.010	0.015	0.025	0.040	0.065	0.10	0.15	0.25	0.40	0.65	1.0	1.5	2.5	4.0	6.5	10	15	25	40	65	100	150	250	400	650	1000
20–29	*	*	*	*	*	*	*	*	*	*	*	*	*	*	*	0	0	2	4	8	14	22	40	68	115	181
30–49	*	*	*	*	*	*	*	*	*	*	*	*	*	*	0	0	1	3	7	13	22	36	63	105	177	277
50–79	*	*	*	*	*	*	*	*	*	*	*	*	0	0	0	2	3	7	14	25	40	63	110	181	301	
80–129	*	*	*	*	*	*	*	*	*	*	*	*	0	0	2	4	7	14	24	42	68	105	181	297		
130–199	*	*	*	*	*	*	*	*	*	*	*	0	0	2	4	8	13	25	42	72	115	177	301	490		
200–319	*	*	*	*	*	*	*	*	*	*	0	0	2	4	8	14	22	40	68	115	181	277	471			
320–499	*	*	*	*	*	*	*	*	*	0	0	1	4	8	14	24	39	68	113	189						
500–799	*	*	*	*	*	*	*	*	0	0	2	3	7	14	25	40	63	110	181							
800–1249	*	*	*	*	*	*	*	0	0	2	4	7	14	24	42	68	105	181								
1250–1999	*	*	*	*	*	*	0	0	2	4	7	13	24	40	69	110	169									
2000–3149	*	*	*	*	*	0	0	2	4	8	14	22	40	68	115	181										
3150–4999	*	*	*	0	0	0	1	4	8	14	24	38	67	111	186											
5000–7999	*	*	*	0	0	2	3	7	14	25	40	63	110	181												
8000–12499	*	*	0	0	2	4	7	14	24	42	68	105	181													
12500–19999	*	0	0	2	4	7	13	24	40	69	110	169														
20000–31499	0	0	2	4	8	14	22	40	68	115	181															
31500–49999	0	1	4	8	14	24	38	67	111	186																
50000 over	2	3	7	14	25	40	63	110	181	301																

*Number of sample units in latest ten lots is insufficient for reduced inspection for these AQLs. In these cases, more than ten lots may be taken into account, but these lots must be a continuation of the latest lots and must have been accepted at the first inspection under the normal inspection plan.

Adjustments of inspections

If you do not make adjustments in inspections under MIL-STD-105D, you will not be benefiting from the advantages of the standard. Yet, it seems that these important adjustments are not carried out very often.

Unless specifically instructed otherwise, the first inspection should be normal. However, when conducting a *normal inspection,* if two lots in five consecutive lots are rejected during the first inspection, change to a *tightened inspection.* When making tightened inspections, if five consecutive lots pass the first inspection, switch to a *normal inspection.* If the latest ten consecutive lots are all accepted after normal inspection or if the number of defectives or defects among the samples is less than the number set as the limit, change to a *reduced inspection.*

When conducting a *reduced inspection,* if there is even one rejection, or if acceptance requires special steps, or production is irregular, change to normal inspection.

Example: MIL-STD-105D is being used for acceptance inspection. The AQL is 2.5 (%), inspection level II, lot size 1,000. Should the single sampling inspection be normal, tightened, or reduced?

Answer: Normal inspection. Looking at table 12.6 for the lot size of 1,000 and an inspection level of II, we find the letter 'J'. Then looking at table 12.7 with 'J' and an AQL of 2.5, we are given the value: $A_c = 5$, $R_e = 6$, and $n = 80$.

For a *tightened inspection* we look at table 12.8, and going across from 'J' for an AQL of 2.5, we are given $A_c = 3$, $R_e = 4$, and $n = 80$. For a *reduced inspection,* we look at table 12.9, and in the same way we learn that $A_c = 2$, $R_e = 5$, and $n = 32$. However, remember here that when $A_c = 2$, even with three or four defectives in the lot it will still be accepted. But you must switch to a normal inspection with the next lot. And, if there are more than five defectives with a reduced inspection, the lot is rejected and the next lot will undergo normal inspection.

There are still many things that could be said about sampling inspection. Although sampling inspections are not particularly difficult, if you are not aware of the basic purposes behind them you can make serious mistakes. Be particularly careful about learning the condition of the quality of the lot. Do not inspect for your convenience. There is always room for improvement, so do not look upon an inspection as perfect. Collect your inspection results and information on the production line which produces the lots, so you can make appropriate revisions in your inspection. Since there are many, many sampling methods, we suggest that you study further. At least we hope you now have a rough idea of what sampling inspection is by means of the examples we have given. Those who wish to study this subject further should consult other books. The examples we have used in our explanation — especially the standard single sampling inspection (JIS-Z-9002) and also MIL-STD-105D — were chosen because they are very common in Japan now.

12.6 Supplementary remarks

Up to now, we have been introducing the common sampling inspection methods conducted in Japan. Following are the categories and the methods:

1 Standard:
   Attributes: JIS Z 9002;
   Variables: JIS Z 9003;
   Variables: JIS Z 9004.
2 With screening:
   Attributes: JIS Z 9006;
   Dodge-Romig.
3 With adjustments:
   Attributes: MIL-STD-105D
   Variables: MIL-STD-414.

Introduced here are the results of a survey on inspection activities in the Japanese firms (from the Third Quality Control Symposium).

(1) Survey of inspection practices

	Receiving (purchase)	Processing (interim)	Final (delivery)	Total
Total inspection	27	46	63	136
JIS Z 9002 (Standard single sampling inspection by attributes)	19	10	18	47
JIS Z 9003 (Standard single sampling inspection by variables, σ known)	25	17	15	57
JIS Z 9004 (Standard single sampling inspection by variables, σ unknown)	6	3	4	13
JIS Z 9006 (Single sampling inspection by attributes with screening)	1	12	10	23
JIS Z 9008 (Sampling inspection for continuous production by attributes)	1	4	5	10
JIS Z 9009 (Standard sequential sampling inspection by attributes)	0	2	1	3
JIS Z 9010 (Standard sequential sampling inspection by variables)	1	0	2	3
JIS Z 9011 (Single sampling inspection with adjustments by attributes)	1	1	1	3
JIS Z 9012 (Single sampling inspection with adjustments by variables)	0	1	0	1
MIL-STD-105A (Sampling inspection with adjustments by attributes)	28	1	14	53
MIL-STD-105D (Sampling inspection with adjustments by attributes)	9	3	6	28
Dodge-Romig (Sampling inspection with screening by attributes)	3	7	6	16
Others (Sampling inspection)	19	18	11	48
Others (Other than sampling inspection such as check inspection)	74	41	31	146
Total	224	176	187	587

(2) Problem areas in sampling inspection

These are just the basic points. For further details, consult standard quality control reference works.

a) Since a sampling inspection samples a part of the whole, the decision reached by this method is for the total lot.

b) The sampling *must* be done at *random,* and this rule must be strictly observed. The proof that your samples represent the lot is the fact that they were selected at random. In order to achieve this, use dice or a table of random numbers.

c) Your decision on the total lot will be based on the results of your examination of the sample. Therefore, if the lot is rejected, you must admit the fact that the lot was rejected and never re-examine the same lot. If you want only good products you must inspect all the products in all the rejected lots. One should never repeat a single sampling by returning the sample and then drawing another sample and, anyway, the chances of acceptance or rejection will remain the same.

For reference sake, examples of sampling tables that refer to similar AQL values are:

MIL-STD-105D (AQL 4%, inspection level II, normal inspection N = 281 ~ 500);

MIL Table II-A (MIL-STD-105D normal inspection single sampling)

$$n = 50, \quad Ac = 5, \quad Re = 6$$

MIL Table III-A* (normal inspection double sampling)

$$n_1 = 32, \quad Ac = 2, \quad Re = 5$$
$$n_2 = 32, \quad Ac = 6, \quad Re = 7$$
$$(n_1 + n_2 = 64)$$

MIL Table IV-A* (normal inspection multiple sampling)

$$n_1 = 13, \quad Ac_1 = \quad Re_1 = 4$$
$$n_2 = 13, \quad Ac_2 = 1, \quad Re_2 = 5$$
$$n_3 = 13, \quad Ac_3 = 2, \quad Re_3 = 6$$
$$n_4 = 13, \quad Ac_4 = 3, \quad Re_4 = 7$$
$$n_5 = 13, \quad Ac_5 = 5, \quad Re_5 = 8$$
$$n_6 = 13, \quad Ac_6 = 7, \quad Re_6 = 9$$
$$n_7 = 13, \quad Ac_7 = 9, \quad Re_7 = 10$$
$$(n_1 + n_2 + n_3 + n_4 + n_5 + n_6 + n_7 = 91)$$

d) The composition of the lot is of crucial importance, since the acceptance or rejection of the lot depends on the samples drawn from it. In this connection, remember the principle of stratification and try to

---

*These tables are not given.

keep together lots based on the same materials, machines, areas, dates of manufacture, etc.

When sampling inspection is erroneous or the results are poor, it is often due to the b) or d) above.

Of course, there is a possibility of having defectives in lots that are accepted. What to do about the defectives in accepted lots is the subject of much debate. Defectives which are found among the sample should be disposed of. However, in practice, products in the samples are being placed back into the accepted lots although they are known to be defective. This should never be done. In addition, defectives from lots that have been accepted and which are being used should be disposed of whenever they are found.

Now we must decide what action to take concerning defective products.

a) Return all defectives to the supplier or manufacturer.

b) Seek reparations from the supplier or manufacturer.

c) Destroy defectives and count them as a loss to your own company.

d) Have defectives repaired in your own plant or by your supplier or manufacturer.

e) If defectives are discovered, inspect all items in the lot.

The items listed above should be clearly settled in business contracts, since they are factors which are likely to come up in inspection. Although they are very important, they are often completely overlooked.

The conditions of the sampling inspection, that is the p_0, p_1, α, β, AOQL (Average Outgoing Quality Level), LTPD (Lot Tolerance Per cent Defective), inspection level and inspection method cannot be changed at will. This should be made clear in the company rules and the procedures for revising these conditions should be established.

Also, giving reasons of shortage of labour, time, inspectors, etc, the size of the sample is often changed. However, sampling inspection is a method founded on the basis of both economy and guarantee of quality, so its principles should never be violated in any way.

If sampling inspection is carried out efficiently, it will economically guarantee product quality.

a) It is more economical than 100 per cent inspection.

b) Product quality can be guaranteed, even in the case of destructive testing.

c) Only a few inspectors are needed.

d) The labour force which would be required for 100 per cent inspection can be used for quality improvement and reduction of defectives.

e) Defectives resulting from inspection (scars, etc) are reduced.

f) As the size of the sample is small, careful and thorough inspection can be accomplished.

g) The inspectors become more careful and more responsible.

h) Lots with poor products are rejected, so the production side takes greater care.

i) Many of the important inspection items can be thoroughly inspected.

j) Chances for omissions in inspection are reduced.

k) Many lots can be inspected with only a few inspectors.

Chapter 13

Practice problems

13.1 How to collect data

(1) In a lens polishing process, two workers have two machines each. The per cent defective has increased recently, so we want to make an investigation. What kind of data should we plan to collect? Set up an appropriate hypothesis.

Since we have not been told about the conditions on the production line or the state of the defective lenses, we will have to make an appropriate hypothesis when we consider the basic points. If you can imagine yourself actually facing these problems, you will find that this helps you carry out your own work smoothly.

As stated in the problem, the purpose is to find the reason for the increase in the per cent defective. So our aims in collecting data will have to be:

    i)   to find out what kind of defectives are most numerous;

    ii) to find what factors are causing the defectives.

The plan must clear up these two points.

(a) Stratify by cause

It is important to obtain data showing the items where most defects occur. In the lens polishing process the lenses may be too thick or too thin, scarred, unfinished, or poorly coated (the lens surface may have been marred by water or acid). It is necessary to collect stratified data to show which of these is most prevalent.

(b) Consider the cause of the defectives

Now it is necessary to find the causes of the above problems. For this, we must make a cause-and-effect diagram. There are many ways of making cause-and-effect diagrams, but the major points that must be remembered are:

    materials used

    effect of parts

    effect of machines and tools

    effect of workers and working group

    effect of work methods

    effect of measurement methods

Naturally, there are many detailed items which can probably be sub-listed under each of the above major points.

(c) Finding the main cause

The method for collecting data must be chosen so as to show the effect of the main cause among all the various causes for defectives. In this problem there are two workers and two machines each, so the data should be collected in such a way as to stratify the effect of the workers and the machines. The data sheet should also be drawn up to facilitate this.

(d) Making a record of related causes

Causal elements that cannot be stratified — for example, materials used, work methods, measurement methods, etc — must be recorded. Make a note of any unusual points concerning them.

Usually the materials and the work methods chosen will be in accordance with the specification standards. However, even within the standards, some effect may be felt, or a standard may no longer be appropriate. In that case it is important to collect data on work conditions and work methods that may be considered important. Even if it is impossible to obtain neat measurement values, data on superiority, data by orders and data expressed in points can still be used to good advantage.

The data measurement method should be recorded as well. Data obtained through sensory tests in particular, such as presence of scars or incompleteness of work, are subject not only to considerable error but become more and more difficult to evaluate as time goes on. Don't forget to note the data collector's name, his tools, when the tools were last checked, etc.

Here is a summary of the above:

    i.   stratify defectives by items
    ii. stratify by worker and machine
    iii. record related factors

An example of a data sheet appears on this page. If you have data from the past and if you analyze them as outlined above, you should be able to obtain a good deal of information.

---

(2) There are a number of things to consider in order to get correct data. List three or more, together with the reasons.

---

a) Make clear the purpose for which the data are to be collected

The purpose for which data are to be collected must be made clear. Data are collected not just to have a record but to provide us with a basis for action. It is therefore important to decide what we are aiming at. Once the aim is determined, we can decide what kind of comparison is to be made, and what kind of data are needed.

Data sheet

Inspector					
Machine number					
Date Data	No. of process	Thickness	Scratches	Chippings	Remarks
Feb. 1					
2					
3					
4					
5					
6					
7					

b) Decide which sampling method to use

After the purpose of data collection has been determined, the next problem is to choose the sampling method. For example, if you wish to investigate the daily per cent defective, it will be necessary to draw samples representing each day's production. If there is almost no dispersion in a day, samples can probably be drawn from anywhere at any time. But, if there is dispersion among workers within a day, then separate samples must be drawn from each worker. The following things must also be decided: what samples you want; how often you want samples; the sampling method (continuous, at intervals, or at random). Nor can you forget the training of the person who is to draw the samples.

c) Be careful of errors in measurement

Even if your samples are selected correctly, you cannot have confidence in any results unless the measuring itself is reliable. So you must be aware of errors in measurement and try to keep them to a minimum. Not only will different instruments give slightly different readings but there will be differences depending on who does the reading and on which days measurements are made. Especially in cases of sensory tests, it is absolutely necessary to know the degree of error in the measurements.

d) Note clearly the origin of the data

Data are collected for many reasons, but in every case make certain that the origin of the data is clear, otherwise later analysis will be impossible. If the data show a cause, then its relationship to effect must be made clear and vice versa. And, of course, always remember to note the date, the instruments, the methods, and the name of the man collecting the data.

e) Be creative when collecting data

Even after deciding on the type of data you need, you will often find that the particular data may be difficult to obtain, that there are no appropriate instruments, or that it is hard to put the data into value figures due to the use of sensory measurements. In such cases, eagerness to collect data will lead to a clue to the solution. Make effective use not only of data that can be easily calculated but also data on superiority, data by orders, and data expressed in points.

13.2 Histograms

(1) The following data represent the measurements of machine parts produced by lines A and B. The tolerance limits are 150 ±0.05 mm. Make a histogram and investigate the relationship between the parts from lines A and B and the boundaries. The values were arrived at by subtracting 150 mm from measured values and then multiplying by 100.

A line						B line					
1	3	2	3	5	4	−1	1	−4	−2	−1	0
1	3	3	4	−1	4	−5	2	3	−1	−2	−1
1	2	0	1	2	−1	0	0	2	0	1	−6
2	3	3	3	2	2	−3	0	−3	1	0	−2
0	1	0	5	3	2	0	1	0	−4	−2	2
0	3	3	2	0	5	−1	0	−1	−3	1	−2
−1	4	2	4	−1	0	−1	1	1	0	−1	2
2	1	1	4	1	7	0	−5	−2	−3	3	−6
4	5	5	3	1	4	2	−1	−4	−1	−2	−2
4	3	−2	2	3	6	−4	−1	−3	0	1	−3

Use the following rules in carrying out your investigation:

i) Make histograms for A and B and for the two combined.

ii) On the basis of the three histograms, check the distribution and investigate its relationship to the boundaries.

iii) Compute the mean values and the standard deviation, and proceed with the investigation.

a) Making histograms

We will use the values for line A in this explanation to illustrate the making of histograms.

Step 1. Count the total number of data (N). $N_A = 60$.

Step 2. On the data table, find the largest value X_L and the smallest X_S. For line A, these are $X_L = 7$, $X_S = -2$.

Step 3. Find the range of the data (R).

$$R = X_L - X_S$$
$$= 7 - (-2)$$
$$= 9$$

Step 4. Decide the width of the class. Total data equals 60, the measurement unit is 1, range is 9. If the *h* width of the class is 1, there can be 9 classes.

Step 5. Check the number of data which belong to each class (/, //, ///, etc). Make a frequency distribution table. Also make a frequency distribution table for B, and another one for A and B combined. This is shown in table 13.1.

Table 13.1 Frequency distribution table

Class representative value	A Line		B Line		A + B
	Tally	Frequency	Tally	Frequency	Frequency
−6			//	2	2
−5			//	2	2
−4			////	4	4
−3			₩₩ /	6	6
−2	/	1	₩₩ ///	8	9
−1	////	4	₩₩ ₩₩ /	11	15
0	₩₩ /	6	₩₩ ₩₩ //	12	18
1	₩₩ ////	9	₩₩ ///	8	17
2	₩₩ ₩₩ /	11	₩₩	5	16
3	₩₩ ₩₩ ///	13	//	2	15
4	₩₩ ////	9			9
5	₩₩	5			5
6	/	1			1
7	/	1			1
		60		60	120

Step 6. If you make a histogram according to the frequency distribution table, it will appear as in figure 13.1. Write in the various lines, the number of data, the mean, the standard deviation, and the boundaries.

146

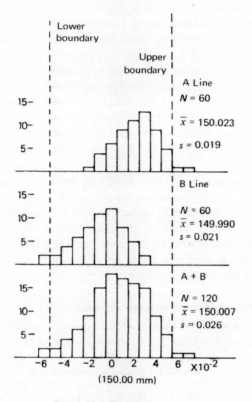

Figure 13.1 Histograms

The line B frequency distribution table can be made in the same way as the one for line A, but the one with both A and B combined should be made with the use of the A and B table. If there is a big difference between the mean of A and B, the number of classes in the frequency distribution table for the two of them will increase.

b) Relationship between distribution and specification

Line A: There is a peak in the measurement of parts at 2 to 3 (150.02 to 150.03 mm) and all 60 data figures are to be found in the range from −2 to 7 (149.98 to 150.07 mm). There is a shift towards the large values from the centre of the boundaries, and the number of defectives in the direction of this shift is two. The distribution is spread out toward the lower boundary, but there are no isolated figures.

Line B: Whereas A's values were spread toward the upper specification boundary, B's values are spread toward the lower boundary. There is a mode around −1 to 0 (149.99 to 150.00 mm) and then there is a spread toward the lower boundary. The data range of the 60 parts is from −6 to 3 (149.94 to 150.03 mm). The dispersion is about the same as A. B has two defectives.

Overall distribution (A plus B): From the above results, the overall central value lies approximately in the centre of the limits. However, because of the difference between the A and B mean values, there is a large dispersion. In addition, the shape of the histogram is a little awkward. (Note that even when there is this big difference in mean values of the A and B lines, the histogram of the combined values does not always show two peaks or modes.)

c) Computing mean $\bar{x}$ and standard deviation s

Use the following problems for reference when computing these values. Make the necessary table for computing for line A (table 13.2).

Table 13.2 Table for computing line A

Class representative value	Frequency f_i	u_i	$f_i u_i$	$f_i u_i^2$
−2 (149.98)	1	−2	−2	4
−1 (149.99)	4	−1	−4	4
0 (150.00)	6	0	(−6)	0
1 (150.01)	9	1	9	9
2 (150.02)	11	2	22	44
3 (150.03)	13	3	39	117
4 (150.04)	9	4	36	144
5 (150.05)	5	5	25	125
6 (150.06)	1	6	6	36
7 (150.07)	1	7	7	49
Total	60		(144) 138	532

Compute $\bar{x}$ and s from the table.

$$\bar{x} = 150.00 + \frac{138}{60} \times 0.01 = 150.023 \text{ (mm)}$$

$$s = 0.01 \sqrt{\frac{532}{60} - (\frac{138}{60})^2}$$

$$= 0.019$$

Line B and lines A and B combined can be computed in the same way. The result is shown in table 13.3 and recorded on the histogram in figure 13.1. First make a chart so that it will be easy to compute these values.

Table 13.3 Mean value and standard deviation

Line	A	B	Overall
Number of observation N	60	60	120
Mean value $\bar{x}$	150.023	149.990	150.007
Standard deviation s	0.019	0.021	0.026

With specifications as 150 ± 0.05 mm, the width of class or class interval is 0.10 mm, or five times the standard deviation (s) of both A and B, roughly 0.020 mm, or nearly four times the overall standard deviation. So that products remain within specifications, the width of class should be at least six times the standard deviation. In terms of process capability index (C_p), it can be expressed thus: $C_p = \dfrac{\text{width of class}}{6s} > 1$. For either line A or B, $C_p \doteqdot 0.83$, and when taking the overall s of A and B, $C_p \doteqdot 0.64$. Both indexes are < 1 so that although products are close to the centre of the specifications, there will still be some defectives.

To eliminate the defectives:

i) Find the reason for the difference between A and B and then try to eliminate it;

ii) Determine how to aim A and B at the centre of the specifications;

iii) Determine how to decrease the dispersion of both A and B. Examine the materials, machinery, workers, work methods and the measurements;

iv) If the dispersion cannot be controlled within the specifications, make a technical examination to see if the class boundaries can be extended.

149

These activities are necessary to improve process capability.

(2) The histogram below shows the weights in grams of 100 samples of a certain food. Find the mean weight of this food and the standard deviation.

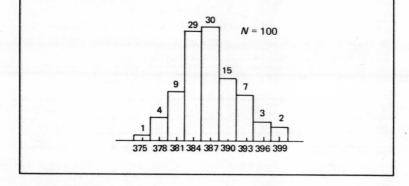

a) How to calculate

Since we are to find the mean weight and the standard deviation based on the histogram, we will first make a chart to simplify our calculation.

Table 13.4

Class number	Class representative value	Frequency f_i	u_i	$f_i u_i$	$f_i u_i^2$
1	375	1	−4	− 4	16
2	378	4	−3	−12	36
3	381	9	−2	−18	36
4	384	29	−1	−29	29
5	387	30	0	(−63)	
6	390	15	1	15	15
7	393	7	2	14	28
8	396	3	3	9	27
9	399	2	4	8	32
Total		100		(46) −17	219

Step 1. Make a table similar to 13.4. The class numbers are taken from the number of bars of the histogram, 1, 2, 3 . . . from the left. A representative value is given to each class. The frequency f_i, which shows the height of the bars, has been recorded. The total of the frequency is 100 (i.e. the number of samples).

Step 2. In the u_i column, 0 has been written as the mean and $-1, -2$, etc were written above that, and 1, 2, etc below that.

Step 3. In every class f_i is multiplied by u_i and the result is in the $f_i u_i$ column. When the u_i value is 0, the column is left blank (do not write in 0). In this example, class number 1 becomes

$$f_i \times u_i = 1 \times (-4) = -4$$

Step 4. Concerning the $f_i u_i$ column where $u_i = 0$, all values above this line are minus and all these are added and written in the 0 line. Their sum is (-63). Below the $u_i - 0$ line all values are positive and total (46). Write this number in the table. Adding these two, we get -17 ($-63 + 46 = -17$).

Step 5. In every class $f_i u_i$ is multiplied by u_i, and the result is put in the $f_i u_i^2$ column. All these values will be positive or 0. For class number 1, it is:

$$f_i u_i \times u_i = (-4) \times (-4) = 16$$

Step 6. Find the total of the $f_i u_i^2$ column. It is 219. Now your preparations for determining the mean value and the standard deviation have been made. Here are the steps showing how to determine them.

Step 7. Take the total of the $f_i u_i$ column that you found in *Step 4* (-17) and divide it by the total number of data (the total of the f_i column: N-100). This will be E_1.

$$E_1 = \frac{-17}{100} = -0.17$$

Step 8. Find the mean with this equation:

$$\bar{x} = a + hE_1$$

Here a is the representative value of the $u_i - 0$ class, h is the width of the class. In this example, $a - 387$ and $h - 3$. Therefore,

$$\bar{x} = 387 + 3 \times (-0.17) = 386.49 \text{ (gm)}$$

Step 9. Divide the total of the $f_i u_i^2$ column which you found in *Step 6* by the total number of data (219). This will be E_2.

$$E_2 = \frac{219}{100} = 2.19$$

Step 10. Find the standard deviation with this equation:

$$s = h\sqrt{E_2 - (E_1)^2}$$

In this example:

$$s = 3\sqrt{2.91 - (-0.17)^2} = 4.41 \text{ (gm)}$$

From the above, we find that the mean value for the weight of this food is 386.49 grams and the standard deviation is 4.41 grams. This mean value is roughly in the centre of the histogram. Also, five times the value of the standard deviation (5 x 4.41 $\doteqdot$ 22) is close to the representative value difference of the biggest and smallest classes (399 − 375 = 24). Therefore, we know there were no big mistakes in calculation.

13.3 Cause-and-effect diagrams

(1) Cooking rice is very similar to a production process in a factory. The rice (raw material) is washed (pretreatment); then, in a pot (equipment), it is heated and steamed (second treatment). Make a cause-and-effect diagram showing the steps necessary to cook good tasting rice.

We had many people work out this problem. The resulting cause-and-effect diagrams they drew are shown in figures 13.2, 13.3, 13.4, 13.5 and 13.6.

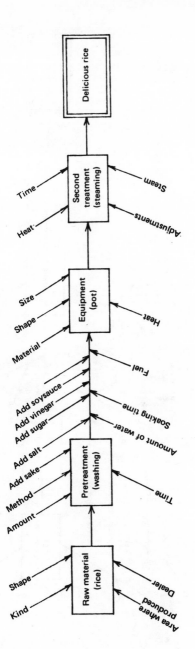

Figure 13.2 Process classification type

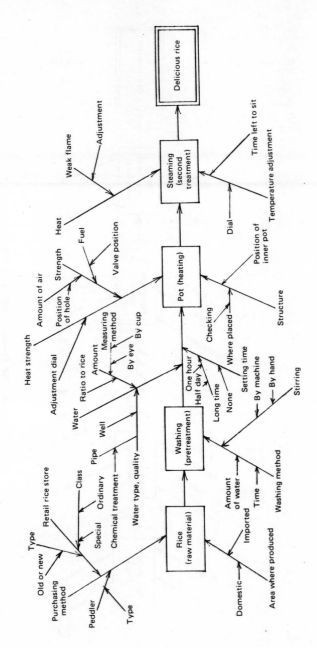

Figure 13.3 Process classification type

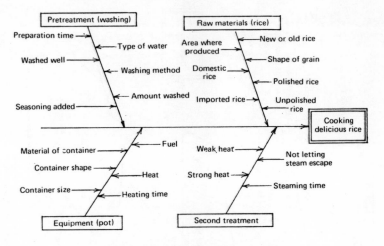

Figure 13.4 Process classification type

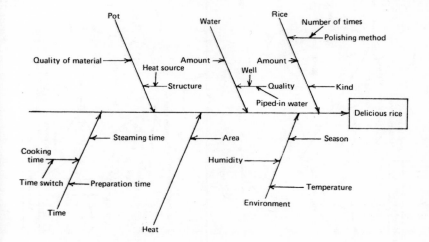

Figure 13.5 Dispersion analysis type

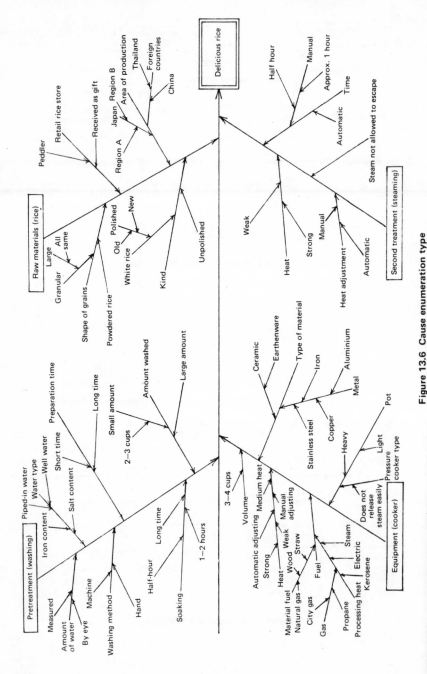

Figure 13.6 Cause enumeration type

Figure 13.2 is a diagram of the process with causes added. It comes under the production process classification type.

Figure 13.3 was done the same way as figure 13.2, except that the causes were listed more completely.

Figure 13.4 is also a process classification type, but the indication of the process has been separated from the central arrow.

Figure 13.5 is of the dispersion analysis type. Here "time" has become a major cause, whereas in the other diagrams it was included as "heating" time, "steaming" time, etc.

Figure 13.6 is of the cause enumeration type. The causes were developed in a brainstorming session.

It is difficult to decide which of these diagrams is best. The person using the diagram will find out which is best. It will be the one that is easiest to use and the one that will serve as a guide to action.

Here are some questions and answers to help illustrate the making of cause-and-effect diagrams.

Question: In the diagrams, both "delicious rice" and "cooking delicious rice" were given as final effects: which one is better?

Answer: This problem concerns "when we cook rice in our homes". The result desired is "delicious rice", so, with regard to the method of attaining that, we use the word "cook". "Delicious rice" is the quality characteristic (effect) and the cooking is the reason (cause). See figure 13.7.

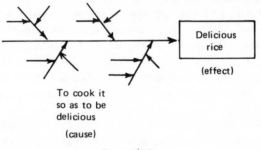

Figure 13.7

As in figure 13.7, the arrows for delicious rice and the cause are combined to form the unit "cooking delicious rice". Therefore, on the right hand side (effect), it will be better to write "delicious rice".

Question: Figures 13.2, 13.3 and 13.4 all come under the production process classification type. Which one is best?

Answer: As we have already mentioned, that will depend on the person using it. However, causes are always intricately interwoven. Where many complicated causes are simplified as in figure 13.2, it will be difficult to take any action. In that respect figure 13.3 is better than figure 13.2. And figure 13.6 is better than figure 13.4.

The length of the production process will influence the ease with which we can use a cause-and-effect diagram. In our experience, we have found that where the line is long and there are many similar causes, a diagram with the process line (figures 13.2, 13.3) is easiest to read. However, for the simple process of cooking rice, figure 13.4 or figure 13.6 is probably better.

Question: What are the differences between the production process classification and the dispersion analysis type diagrams?

Answer: The dispersion analysis type is made as an answer to the question, why dispersion occurs. If the cause is thought to be in the production process, then the main causes (factors) are drawn in as large branches as in figures 13.4 and 13.6. In figure 13.5, the causes were roughly classified into rice, water, pot, time, heat and environment.

As previously stated, in figures 13.4 and 13.5 all the time factors are listed here under "time". However, time is also involved in each step: washing, heating and steaming, etc. So there is a question, how to classify a cause that appears many times.

Question: With an electric rice cooker, heat and time are all automatically controlled. What do you do in this case?

Answer: Figure 13.5 was made with an automatic cooker in mind. Figure 13.6 is for any cooking pot or method. We must consider the causes of dispersion within the limitations that exist. If an automatic cooker is the only one we have, then we must consider the best way of working within that limitation, and omit considerations applicable to gas or other cookers.

Question: Isn't a diagram such as figure 13.6 too complicated to work with?

Answer: Yes. And cause that has no real effect on the result should be completely removed. A good diagram is one that is easy to use and which leads to action.

---

(2) Make a cause-and-effect diagram for improving your factory quality control group.

We had many people complete this problem. Two representative diagrams are shown here. Use them in your group and see which is best (figures 13.8, 13.9).

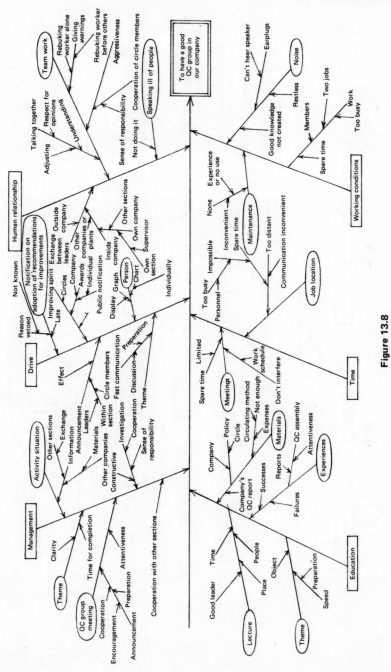

Figure 13.8

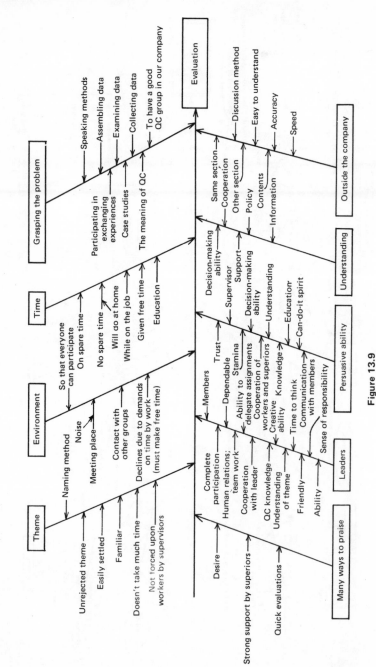

Figure 13.9

160

13.4 Check sheets

(1) What points must we be careful of in designing a check sheet?

a) Fully understand the purpose

As you saw in chapter 4, check sheets can be used for many purposes. But we can divide them into two main groups: check sheets for the production process and check sheets for check-up and confirmation. Since the reasons for using the two are basically different, we can think about them separately. We will first take up the check sheet for production process.

    i) What do you want to know and what do you have to investigate?

    ii) On the basis of the results, what action will you take?

If these two points are understood, you will automatically know how data should be collected.

b) Check sheets must have detailed stratified information

If the purpose is fully understood, you will then know how to stratify your information. If your check sheet is for analyzing the process, you'll need stratified information on the following: workers, machines, equipment, materials, shifts, times, dates, products, and others. All these should be listed clearly on the check sheet. Either they can be recorded on each sheet or the information can be recorded separately on different coloured paper. Check sheets for control of the process are used in a similar manner. When unusual conditions occur in the process, stratified information is necessary to find the cause. What kinds of materials were in use, which machines, which workers, etc? If this sort of information can be obtained from the check sheet, then it will not be so difficult to trace the trouble.

c) Make the data as easy to collect as possible

Check sheets are tools to simplify data collection. If you try to put too much information on check sheets, you will find they are too hard to use. A check sheet should list only the most essential information. This may seem to contradict the above, but it does not. First of all, only study those things you regard as most important and then, if that is not enough, expand your field of study. But, at all stages, the purposes for stratification must always be clearly understood.

161

For checking and approving check sheets, remember the following:

  i) Make certain that no check or test is omitted from the sheet. The check sheet itself must be accurate and complete, since the checking will be based on this sheet.

  ii) Be careful in lining up the various checks to be made on the sheet.

See to it that the items on the check sheet are listed in the same sequence as the processes are actually performed; it saves time and labour. On check sheets for equipment maintenance, list all daily checks together, all weekly checks together, and so on, since the frequency for checking them will be different. It may also be good to put a circle around the most important checks.

---

(2) Analyze the data given in figure 13.10.

---

a) First, a Pareto diagram prepared on the basis of the information given in figure 13.10 will appear as in figure 13.11. It can be seen that more than half the defects are surface scratches.

	Worker	Mon. AM	Mon. PM	Tues. AM	Tues. PM	Wed. AM	Wed. PM	Thur. AM	Thur. PM	Fri. AM	Fri. PM	Sat. AM	Sat. PM
Machine 1	A	oox•	ox	ooo	oxx	ooox xx•	oooo xxx	oooo x••	oxx	oooo	oo	o	xx•
Machine 1	B	oxx•	ooox x•	oooo ooxx	ooox x	oooo ooxx •	oooo ooxx•	oooo oxx	ooox ••	ooxx •	oooo o	oox	ooo• xox
Machine 2	C	oox	ox	oo	•	oooo o	oooo oox	oo	o•	ooΔ	ooo	Δo	oo
Machine 2	D	oox	ox	ooΔ	ooo•	ooo• Δ	oooo ox	o•o	ooΔΔ □	ooΔ	o••	□oox	xxo

Figure 13.10

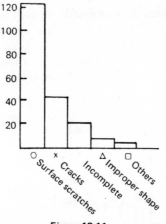

Figure 13.11

b) Next, Pareto diagrams made for machines No. 1 and No. 2 will appear as in figure 13.12. It can be assumed that the nature of the defects for machine No. 1 differs from that of machine No. 2. There are many surface scratches and cracks on products from machine No. 1. In particular, cracks are more numerous in the case of machine No. 1 than No. 2. But machine No. 2 has seven improper shape defects whereas No. 1 has none.

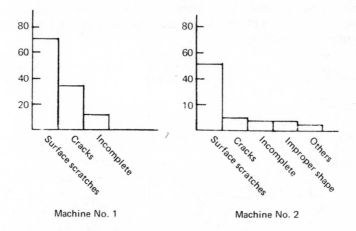

Machine No. 1   Machine No. 2

Figure 13.12

163

c) Furthermore, Pareto diagrams made for each worker look as in figure 13.13. Worker B produces the most surface scratches. As mentioned in chapter 4, this is because he was not operating his machine properly. On the basis of this data alone, it cannot be determined if the cracks from machine No. 1 are the fault of the machine or the worker. An on-the-spot study will be necessary.

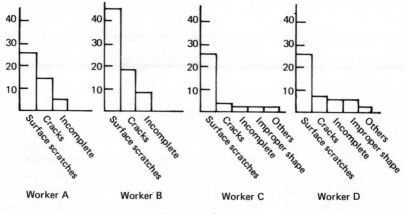

Figure 13.13

d) Pareto diagrams for the morning and the afternoon will be like the ones in figure 13.14. It can be seen that there is not a great deal of difference between the two.

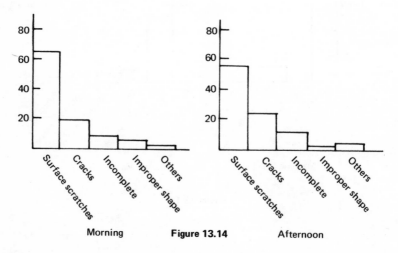

Morning   **Figure 13.14**   Afternoon

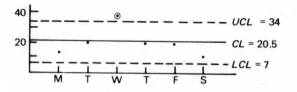

Figure 13.15 *c* **control chart**

e) Figure 13.15 is the surface control chart for one week. On Wednesday, scratches went beyond the limit. This was due to faulty materials.

The following conclusions could be drawn:

i) The most frequent defect is surface scratches.

- The relationship between improper machine operation and surface scratches was analyzed and corrections made.
- Faulty materials were found to affect the occurrence of surface scratches. Stricter materials control is needed.
- The rest of the scratches will be charted on a cause-and-effect diagram and the reasons studied.

ii) The frequency of cracks differs between machines No. 1 and No. 2. With this data alone it is not possible to determine whether the problem lies in the equipment or the workers. Further study is necessary.

iii) Machine No. 2 is the only one with improper shape defects. This cause will be further studied.

13.5 Pareto diagrams

> (1) Table 13.5 gives data on defectives taken from a certain assembly line over a one month period. With which items should improvement begin?

Prepare a Pareto diagram and decide where improvement must begin. The table gives the number of defectives for a period of one month (four weeks). To make a Pareto diagram based on this data, first find the total number of defectives for each item.

Table 13.6 is exactly the same as table 13.5 except that the totals have been computed and added on the far right side.

Your Pareto diagram should resemble the one given in figure 13.16. From this chart we see that "improper rotation" and "base panel breaks" must be corrected first.

> (2) Make changes in the data time factor and prepare corresponding Pareto diagrams. Consider the manner in which the defectives appear over this one month period and the time limits for collecting the data.

In the first question we have learned about the corrections for improper rotation and base panel breaks, with a Pareto diagram based on data for a one month period. Since we are given four weeks worth of data for this problem, we can make four diagrams (one for each week) or two diagrams (one for every two weeks).

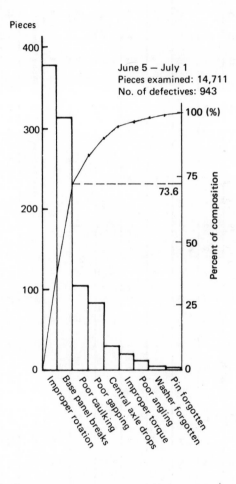

Figure 13.16 Pareto diagram showing rejects for one month (four weeks)

Table 13.5

Date June	5	6	7	8	9	10	12	13	14	15	16	17	19	20	21	22	23	24	26	27	28	29	30	July 1
Poor caulking	3		6	14	18	15	2	4	3	3	4	2	3	5	2	6	2	2			1	3	3	4
Improper rotation	15	18	14	14	19	13	14	16	20	23	19	17	17	13	12	15	15	17	13	19	11	12	18	14
Improper torque		3				1	2				5				4	2				1	1	1		
Poor gapping	5	1	4	4	1	3	5	8	6	3	3	7	3	7	2	3	1		3	2	6	4		2
Base panel breaks	8	11	7	16	6	9	7	7	13	10	21	26	10	14	9	8	15	8	8	31	19	23	16	12
Poor angling			1		2				1		1		1	1						2		1		1
Central axle drops	2	1	4	3				1	1				2						3	3	1	4	2	1
Others				1 (Pin forgotten)										1 (Washer forgotten)							1 (Washer forgotten)			
Total	33	34	36	52	46	41	30	36	44	39	54	52	36	41	29	34	33	27	27	58	40	48	39	34
Units produced	615	631	607	621	599	611	610	615	611	608	595	603	620	621	615	613	620	614	628	607	609	622	615	601

(Defects)

Table 13.6 Assembly line defectives

	Date June	5	6	7	8	9	10	12	13	14	15	16	17	19	20	21	22	23	24	26	27	28	29	30	July 1	Total
Defects	Poor caulking	3	6	6	14	18	15	2	4	3	3	4	2	3	5	2	6	2	2			1	3	3	4	105
	Improper rotation	15	18	14	14	19	13	14	16	20	23	19	17	17	13	12	15	15	17	13	19	11	12	18	14	378
	Improper torque		3				1	2				5			4		2				1	1	1			20
	Poor gapping	5	1	4	4	1	3	5	8	6	3	3	7	3	7	2	3	1		3	2	6	4	2	2	83
	Base panel breaks	8	11	7	16	6	9	7	7	13	10	21	26	10	14	9	8	15	8	8	31	19	23	16	12	314
	Poor angling			1		2				1		1		1	1						2		1		1	11
	Central axle drops	2	1	4	3				1	1		1		2						3	3	1	4	2	1	29
	Others			(Pin forgotten) 1											(Washer forgotten) 1			(Washer forgotten) 1				(Washer forgotten) 1				3
	Total	33	34	36	52	46	41	30	36	44	39	54	52	36	41	29	34	33	27	27	58	40	48	39	34	943
	Units produced	615	631	607	621	599	611	610	615	611	608	595	603	620	621	615	613	620	614	628	607	609	622	615	601	14,711

169

To find the manner in which the defectives appear in one month we will have to compare diagrams. Therefore, set the time limits at one week and two weeks. If we set the time limits at three weeks and one week for the four weeks worth of data, we would not be able to compare diagrams. (For references, see chapter 5, paragraph 5.2, step 2.)

Table 13.7 First week

	Date	June / 5	6	7	8	9	10	Total
Defects	Poor caulking	3		6	14	18	15	56
	Improper rotation	15	18	14	14	19	13	93
	Improper torque		3				1	4
	Poor gapping	5	1	4	4	1	3	18
	Base panel breaks	8	11	7	16	6	9	57
	Poor angling			1		2		3
	Central axle drops	2	1	4	3			10
	Others				(Pin forgotten) 1			1
	Total	33	34	36	52	46	41	242
	Units produced	615	631	607	621	599	611	3684

Table 13.8 Second week

12	13	14	15	16	17	Total
2	4	3	3	4	2	18
14	16	20	23	19	17	109
2				5		7
5	8	6	3	3	7	32
7	7	13	10	21	26	84
		1		1		2
	1	1		1		3
						0
30	36	44	39	54	52	255
610	615	611	608	595	603	3642

Table 13.9 Third week

19	20	21	22	23	24	Total
3	5	2	6	2	2	20
17	13	12	15	15	17	89
		4	2			6
3	7	2	3	1		16
10	14	9	8	15	8	64
1	1					2
2						2
	(Washer forgotten) 1					1
36	41	29	34	33	27	200
620	621	615	613	620	614	3703

Table 13.10 Fourth week

26	27	28	29	30	July / 1	Total
		1	3	3	4	11
13	19	11	12	18	14	87
	1	1	1			3
3	2	6	4		2	17
8	31	19	23	16	12	109
	2		1		1	4
3	3	1	4	2	1	14
		(Washer forgotten) 1				1
27	58	40	48	39	34	246
628	607	609	622	615	601	3682

Tables 13.7 to 13.10 give the weekly totals of defectives, daily totals of defectives, and production totals. If we add the totals for the first week and the second week, we will have the basis for our first Pareto diagram. The totals for the third and fourth weeks will give us our second. These diagrams are shown in figure 13.17 (A) and 13.17 (B).

In both of these diagrams, the position of the two leading defective causes ("improper rotation" and "base panel breaks") is the same, occupying 73.6% of the total defectives. The positions of "poor caulking" and "poor gapping" have changed, but in comparing the first half of the month with the latter half on the basis of these two diagrams, we find there is really not a great deal of difference in the manner in which the defectives appear.

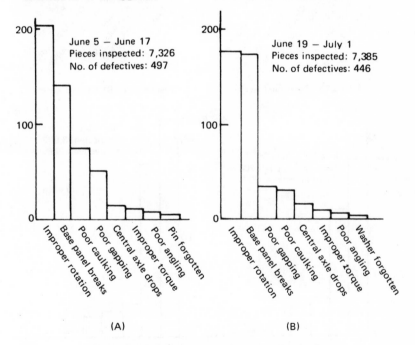

Figure 13.17 Pareto diagrams for two-week periods

Comparing the two diagrams we find the results the same as in figure 13.16 — that is, improper rotation and base panel breaks must be corrected. The Pareto diagrams for each week are shown in figures 13.18 (A) to 13.18 (D)

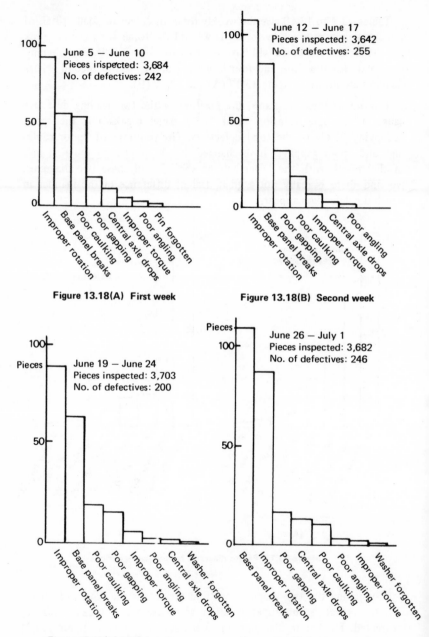

Figure 13.18(A) First week

Figure 13.18(B) Second week

Figure 13.18(C) Third week

Figure 13.18(D) Fourth week

172

Table 13.11 Changes in order

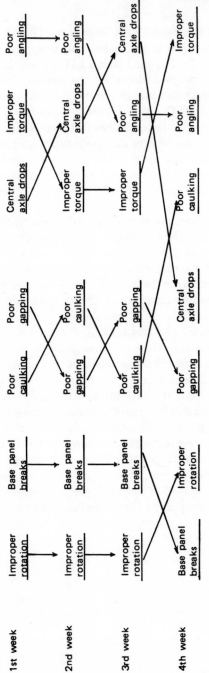

We see that in the fourth week "improper rotation", which had been in the first place, dropped to the second and "base panel breaks" moved up to the first place. By preparing table 13.11, we will find that this was not the only change in order (shown by the arrows). The more the arrows cross and the longer they are, the greater the lack of daily quality control on the assembly line. Thus we can learn that the changes encountered on a weekly basis, as in this factory, mean that there is little daily control. The diagram made on the basis of data for a two week period (figure 13.17) did not reveal these changes very well. However, with the graphs made for each week, the changes are quite clear. As control improves, the length of the arrows and the number of times they cross in tables made for each week will decrease.

Using Pareto diagrams in this way will reveal whether the control is suitable or not. The shortest amount of time needed for the data will vary in each case, but in general a week is considered a minimum. With such problems as this, the time limit can be set at three days. But, if we do so, there will be times when the number of defectives will be zero. The period needed for collecting data can be roughly estimated on the basis of a period when all the main defectives appear.

Note: In figures 13.17 and 13.18, the vertical axis stands for the number of defectives. This was done because the number of pieces inspected in the diagrams being compared was nearly the same. If there had been a big difference in the number of pieces inspected, it would be necessary to calculate the per cent defective and, with a Pareto diagram having its vertical axis in per cent (%), compare the two.

If we examine "improper rotation", for example, we will see that the number of defectives each week is not constant: 93, 109, 89, 87.

For each item in the defective causes, daily changes in the number of defectives can also be seen. if we study these changes using the control chart which is explained in chapter 7, the effectiveness of the control can be seen more clearly than by comparing Pareto diagrams.

13.6 Graphs

Below you will find data on defectives collected during the production process in the month of April at a certain electrical manufacturer (producing mainly stereo equipment).

1 From this data, make a pie diagram, a bar graph and a Pareto diagram of the respective items and the responsible sections.

2 Analyze the information drawn from the data.

Item	Number	Responsible section
Vacuum tube	327	Electronics subsidiary A
Pilot lamp	240	Purchasing section
Transistor	176	Electronics subsidiary B
Neon tube	105	Purchasing section
Speaker	90	Speaker plant
Coil (A)	61	Coil plant
Rotary switch	21	Assembly parts plant
Volume control	15	Volume control maker
Carbon resistance	14	Resistor plant
Diode	14	Electronics subsidiary B
Condenser (C)	12	Purchasing section
Transformer (B)	10	Transformer plant
Condenser (D)	9	Purchasing section
Variable condenser	8	Purchasing section
Condenser (A)	50	Condenser plant
Condenser (B)	45	Condenser plant
Headphone jack	43	Purchasing section
Transformer	36	Coil plant
Coil (B)	33	Coil plant
Six-spool trimmer	31	Purchasing section
Coil	8	Coil plant
Seesaw switch	8	Assembly parts plant
Solid state resistor	8	Solid state resistor plant
Transformer (C)	7	Transistor plant
Slide switch	6	Assembly parts plant
Printed circuit	2	Printed circuit plant
Composite parts	1	Ceramic plant
Others	23	

Item	Number of rejects	Responsible section
Vacuum tube	327	Electronics subsidiary A
Pilot lamp	240	Purchasing section
Transistor	176	Electronics subsidiary B
Neon tube	105	Purchasing section
Speaker	90	Speaker plant
Coil (A)	61	Coil plant
Condenser (A)	50	Condenser plant
Condenser (B)	45	Condenser plant
Headphone jack	43	Purchasing section
Transformer	36	Transistor plant
Coil (B)	33	Coil plant
Six-spool trimmer	31	Purchasing section
Rotary switch	21	Assembly parts plant
Volume	15	Volume plant
Carbon resistor	14	Resistor plant
Diode	14	Electronics subsidiary B
Condenser (C)	12	Purchasing section
Transformer (B)	10	Transformer plant
Condenser (D)	9	Purchasing section
Variable condenser	8	Purchasing section
Coil (C)	8	Coil plant
Seesaw switch	8	Assembly parts plant
Solid state resistor	8	Resistor plant
Transformer C	7	Transformer plant
Slide switch	6	Assembly parts plant
Printed circuit	2	Printed circuit plant
Composite parts	1	Ceramics plant
Others	23	
Total	1,403	

Separate items

Itemwise

Item	Number	Item	Number
Vacuum tube	327	Condenser (B)	45
Pilot lamp	240	Headphone jack	43
Transistor	176	Transformer (A)	36
Neon tube	105	Coil (B)	33
Speaker	90	Six-spool trimmer	31
Coil (A)	61	Others	166
Condenser (A)	50	Total	1,403

Productwise

Item	Number	Item	Number
Vacuum tube	327	Transformer	53
Pilot lamp	240	Headphone jack	43
Transistor	176	Six-spool trimmer	31
Condenser	116	Rotary switch	21
Neon tube	105	Volume	15
Coil	102	Others	84
Speaker	90	Total	1,403

Responsible section

Responsible sectionwise

Related section	Number
Purchasing section	448
Electronics subsidiary A	327
Electronics subsidiary B	190
Coil plant	102
Condenser plant	95
Speaker plant	90
Transformer plant	53
Others	98

Itemwise within responsible sections

Related section	Item	Number
Purchasing section (448)	Pilot lamp	240
	Neon tube	105
	Headphone jack	43
	Six-spool trimmer	31
	Condenser (C) (D)	21
	Variable condenser	8
Electronics subsidiary B (190)	Transistor	176
	Diode	14
Coil plant (102)	Coil (A)	61
	Coil (B)	33
	Coil (C)	8
Condenser plant (95)	Condenser (A)	50
	Condenser (B)	45

Figure 13.19

176

After the data have been gathered, they can be put to practical use by clarifying the aim and method of selecting the appropriate data and relating them to the required use.

What was the purpose for gathering the data? For instance, try to connect the information with concrete action; rearrange it in easy-to-read language, inform your subordinates, report to your superiors for further instructions etc. Consequently, the method for using, writing and observing (with regard to data) is as follows.

a) Data analysis (stratification)

First of all, let's stratify the data according to both item and responsible production section (see figure 13.19).

Another method of analysis consists of separating the data into groups such as circuit parts, assembly parts, etc.

Summary

1 Consider exactly what types of data are required, and collect data for your specific purpose.
2 Stratify the data.
3 All data should represent facts. Eliminate false data from the workshop.
4 Examine the reliability of the data.
5 When there are numerous defective items, check to what extent in detail data were collected.

b) Making itemwise pie charts, bar graphs and Pareto diagrams

i) Making pie charts

Pie charts are easier to read than graphs, but it is difficult to tell at a glance what the proportions are between the area of one "slice of pie" and the others. The easiest way to make a pie chart is to use a circle and divide its circumference into 100 equal parts (see figure 13.20). Once you know the percentage of the total accounted for by each item, it is a simple matter to prepare the pie chart.

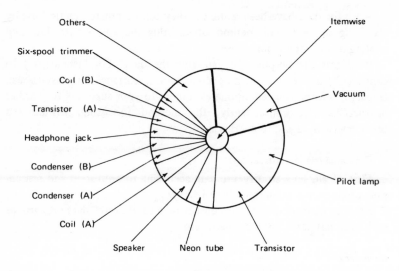

Figure 13.20

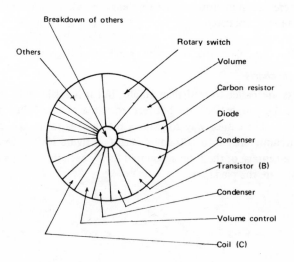

Figure 13.21

The other method requires a simple arithmetical calculation to express each item in terms of degrees. In this case, a protractor is used to draw the chart. The calculations are as follows:

$$\text{Vacuum tube} \ldots \ldots \ldots \ldots \ldots 360° \times \frac{327}{1403} = 87°$$

$$\text{Pilot lamp} \ldots \ldots \ldots \ldots \ldots 360° \times \frac{240}{1403} = 61.8°$$

$$\text{Transistor} \ldots \ldots \ldots \ldots \ldots 360° \times \frac{176}{1403} = 45°$$

$$\text{Neon tube} \ldots \ldots \ldots \ldots \ldots 360° \times \frac{105}{1403} = 27°$$

$$\text{Speaker} \ldots \ldots \ldots \ldots \ldots 360° \times \frac{90}{1403} = 23°$$

$$\text{Coil (A)} \ldots \ldots \ldots \ldots \ldots 360° \times \frac{61}{1403} = 15.7°$$

$$\text{Condenser} \ldots \ldots \ldots \ldots \ldots 360° \times \frac{50}{1403} = 12.8°$$

$$\text{Condenser (B)} \ldots \ldots \ldots \ldots 360° \times \frac{45}{1403} = 11.5°$$

$$\text{Headphone jack} \ldots \ldots \ldots \ldots 360° \times \frac{43}{1403} = 11°$$

$$\text{Transformer (A)} \ldots \ldots \ldots \ldots 360° \times \frac{36}{1403} = 9.2°$$

$$\text{Coil (B)} \ldots \ldots \ldots \ldots \ldots 360° \times \frac{33}{1403} = 8.5°$$

$$\text{Six-spool trimmer} \ldots \ldots \ldots 360° \times \frac{31}{1403} = 7.9°$$

$$\text{Others} \ldots \ldots \ldots \ldots \ldots 360° \times \frac{166}{1403} = 42.6°$$

ii) Composition of the bar graph

The bar graph is used considerably in our daily life. It is used for comparing values shown by variations in the lengths of the bars. The difference and ratio of each quantity must be taken into consideration when making comparisons.

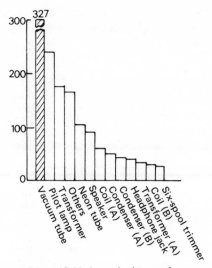

Figure 13.22 Itemwise bar graph

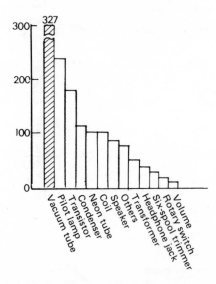

Figure 13.23 Productwise bar graph

iii) Making a Pareto diagram

The Pareto diagram is also a kind of bar graph and is frequently used for weighing the importance of problems at the workshop. Although there are usually numerous defective items or causes at the workshop, only two or three of these items or causes will generally have a significant influence.

To make a Pareto diagram, determine the percentage of each type of defective within the whole, and draw a bar for each. Also write in a line showing the cumulative totals of the values for each item.

For each item, the calculation is as follows:

Vacuum tube . . . . $\frac{327}{1403} \times 100\% = 23.2\%$

Pilot lamp . . . . $\frac{240}{1403} \times 100\% = 17.1\%$

Transistor . . . . $\frac{176}{1403} \times 100\% = 12.5\%$

Neon tube . . . . $\frac{105}{1403} \times 100\% = 7.5\%$

Headphone jack . . . . $\frac{43}{1403} \times 100\% = 3.1\%$

Transformer (A) . . . . $\frac{36}{1403} \times 100\% = 2.6\%$

Transformer (B) . . . . $\frac{33}{1403} \times 100\% = 2.4\%$

Speaker . . . . $\frac{90}{1403} \times 100\% = 6.4\%$

Coil (A) . . . . $\frac{61}{1403} \times 100\% = 4.4\%$

Condenser . . . . $\frac{50}{1403} \times 100\% = 3.6\%$

Condenser (B) . . . . $\frac{45}{1403} \times 100\% = 3.2\%$

Six-spool trimmer . . . . $\frac{31}{1403} \times 100\% = 2.2\%$

Others . . . . $\frac{166}{1403} \times 100\% = 11.8\%$

Summary

Pie charts, bar graphs and Pareto diagrams have been drawn for each defective item. As may be seen in charts and graphs, and also in statistics, the numbers of defective vacuum tubes, pilot lamps and transistors are highest, although the values of some items may be different according to the method of stratification. Nevertheless, it is necessary to sum up the data according to one's aims, to give information to your subordinates (using a pie chart or bar graphs) and to determine the course of action needed for improvement (using a Pareto diagram).

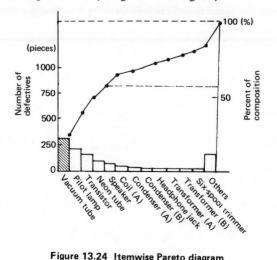

Figure 13.24 Itemwise Pareto diagram

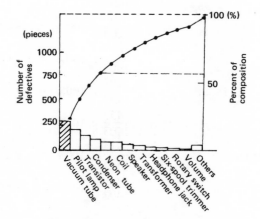

Figure 13.25 Productwise Pareto diagram

c) Making pie charts, bar graphs and Pareto diagrams for each responsible section

Try to make a graph or chart such as in figures 13.26 and 13.27. The same methods as those used in making the itemwise graphs can be applied here.

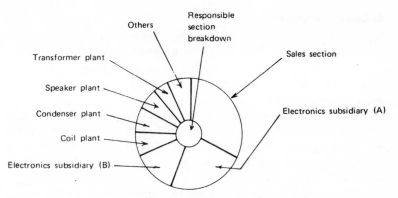

Figure 13.26 Pie chart

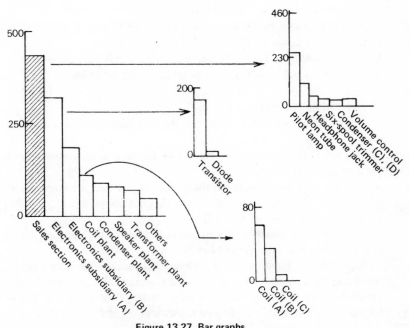

Figure 13.27 Bar graphs

183

Summary

Pie charts, bar graphs or Pareto diagrams have been drawn for the responsible sections as well as the items; each of them must be made to conform to its specific aims. In this case, it is also necessary to stratify and analyze those items which are numerous in each responsible section.

d) General summary

i) It is difficult to absorb at a glance the total state of affairs with regard to data. Moreover, although it is rather troublesome, one should make it a daily habit to chart the data according to one's aims (to give information to your subordinates, to report the information to your superiors, or to apply the data as control factors).

ii) If you analyze in detail the items which account for a relatively large per cent defective, it will be much easier to reach the target you have set.

iii) When numerous defective items are found, figure out how to determine the items to concentrate on, and how to stratify before finally analyzing the data.

iv) When defective items of relatively low importance can be improved at minimum cost and time, action should be taken as soon as possible.

v) Another way of evaluating data (with relation to a time system) is to compare them with those of the previous month.

vi) If the data can be expressed in amounts of money, it will be more effective to put down the data values in monetary terms.

vii) When making a chart it is useful to have a crayon, pen, or marker handy, to make bold, thick lines to emphasize a certain point.

e) Information acquired

After making the various analyses, the following information can be obtained.

i) Vacuum tubes, pilot lamps, transistors and neon tubes account for 60 per cent of all defectives.

ii) In the responsible sections, the purchasing section accounts for 40 per cent of all defectives, among which pilot lamps and neon tubes account for 77 per cent of the total.

iii) Compare this month's information with that for the previous month to see whether any improvement has been made.

From the above results, it is discovered that vacuum tubes, pilot lamps, transistors and neon tubes predominate among the defective items. Concentrate on these four as your target, arrange the items that will be targets in each section, including your own section, and take the necessary action for improvement.

It was considered seeing to what extent an analysis could be made by using pie diagrams and bar graphs. It may seem easy enough to gather a maximum of information from a simple statistical graph and then take the appropriate action. Yet this is not fully practised. Check and see at what level your analyzing ability lies.

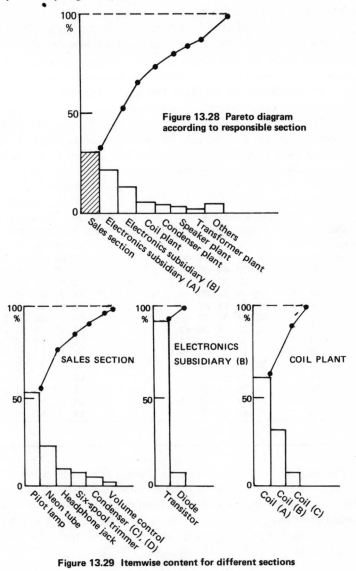

Figure 13.28 Pareto diagram according to responsible section

Figure 13.29 Itemwise content for different sections

13.7 Control charts 1

This exercise deals with a certain mechanical part that is machined by using a lathe. Defective hole diameters have recently been found in these parts, and the defects have had an adverse effect on assembly work. We have data from a daily random sampling of the diameter of holes of five parts from the production process.

1 The data below are the latest that have been collected. On the basis of these data, construct a control chart.

2 The material used was changed at the end of September. Make control charts for the two materials and study the influence of the material used on hole diameter. The data in the following table have been simplified for easier calculation.

Date	Material	Hole diameter data (unit: 0.001mm)					Date	Material	Hole diameter data (unit: 0.001mm)				
Sept. 14	F	7	24	24	20	25	Oct. 3	K	37	19	39	21	38
15	"	17	37	28	16	26	4	"	37	46	22	26	25
16	"	12	22	40	36	34	5	"	13	32	35	56	45
17	"	52	35	29	36	24	6	"	9	51	25	37	39
19	"	28	28	34	29	48	7	"	14	27	34	37	52
20	"	39	27	48	32	25	8	"	30	51	34	36	28
21	"	36	21	31	22	28	10	"	54	31	35	29	25
22	"	5	33	15	26	42	11	"	45	21	38	38	31
23	"	50	34	37	27	34	12	"	19	31	27	25	38
24	"	21	17	20	25	16	13	"	25	45	41	36	43
26	"	34	18	29	43	24	14	"	30	24	44	48	38
27	"	18	35	26	23	17	15	"	64	32	32	42	42
28	"	10	28	19	26	21	17	"	8	58	65	33	39
29	"	21	23	35	28	38	18	"	38	37	50	37	33
30	"	27	41	15	22	23	19	"	64	38	47	49	41

The purpose of this exercise is to study the possible causes of the drilling defects using a *control chart for process analysis*. As explained above, first make the control chart from the total data. Then make a control chart stratified for the two materials. Analyze the data that have been provided by both charts and summarize them for further consideration.

a) Control chart using total data

In this exercise, five units of data are obtained every day, so we'll regard them as one sub-group. In other words, the size of the sub-group is $n = 5$ and the number of sub-groups is $k = 30$. As the data have already been entered on a proper data sheet, make columns for the total value in each sub-group, mean values $\bar{x}$, and range R on the right side of the data sheet and write in the results calculated.

Refer to paragraph 7.3 of chapter 7 and make your calculations as follows:

Step 1. Total the values of each sub-group.

For instance, the initial sub-group for September 14 shows:

$$7 + 24 + 24 + 20 + 25 = 100$$

Total the subsequent values (data) in the sub-groups as well and write them down on the data sheet (see table 13.12).

Step 2. Find the mean value $\bar{x}$.

For instance, the initial sub-group shows:

$$\bar{x} = 100/5 = 20.0$$

Also, find the subsequent sub-groups and put the results down on the data sheet.

Step 3. Find the range R.

For instance, the initial sub-group is represented by:

$$R = 25 - 7 = 18$$

Also, find the subsequent sub-groups and put the results down on the data sheet.

Step 4. Find the overall mean $\bar{\bar{x}}$.

$$\bar{\bar{x}} = \frac{20.0 + 24.8 + \cdots + 47.8}{30} = \frac{954.2}{30} \approx 31.81$$

Step 5. Find the average value of the range $\bar{R}$.

$$\bar{R} = \frac{18 + 21 + \ldots + 26}{30} = \frac{764}{30} \approx 25.5$$

Step 6. Compute the control limit lines.

187

Table 13.12 Data sheet

Date		Mate-rial	Hole diameter (unit: 0.001mm)					Total	$\bar{x}$	R
Sept.	14	F	7	24	24	20	25	100	20.0	18
	15	"	17	37	28	16	26	124	24.8	21
	16	"	12	22	40	36	34	144	28.8	28
	17	"	52	35	29	36	24	176	35.2	28
	19	"	28	28	34	29	48	167	33.4	20
	20	"	39	27	48	32	25	171	34.2	23
	21	"	36	21	31	22	28	138	27.6	15
	22	"	5	33	15	26	42	121	24.2	37
	23	"	50	34	37	27	34	182	36.4	23
	24	"	21	17	20	25	16	99	19.8	9
	26	"	34	18	29	43	24	148	29.6	25
	27	"	18	35	26	23	17	119	23.8	18
	28	"	10	28	19	26	21	104	20.8	18
	29	"	21	23	35	28	38	145	29.0	17
	30	"	27	41	15	22	23	128	25.6	26
Oct.	3	K	37	19	39	21	38	154	30.8	20
	4	"	37	46	22	26	25	156	21.2	24
	5	"	13	32	35	56	45	181	36.2	43
	6	"	9	51	25	37	39	161	32.2	42
	7	"	14	27	34	37	52	164	32.8	38
	8	"	30	51	34	36	28	179	35.8	23
	10	"	54	31	35	29	25	174	34.8	29
	11	"	45	21	38	38	31	173	34.6	24
	12	"	19	31	27	25	38	140	28.0	19
	13	"	25	45	41	36	43	190	38.0	20
	14	"	30	24	44	48	38	184	36.8	24
	15	"	64	32	32	42	42	212	42.4	32
	17	"	8	58	65	33	39	203	40.6	57
	18	"	38	37	50	37	33	195	39.0	17
	19	"	64	38	47	49	41	239	47.8	26

Grand Total 954.2   764

$\bar{x}$ control chart:

Centre line $\qquad$ CL $= \bar{\bar{x}} = 31.81$

Upper control limit UCL $= \bar{\bar{x}} + A_2\bar{R} = 31.81 + 0.577 \times 25.5$
$$\approx 31.81 + 14.71$$
$$= 46.52$$

Lower control limit LCL $= \bar{\bar{x}} - A_2 R = 31.81 - 0.577 \times 25.5$
$$\approx 31.81 - 14.71$$
$$= 17.10$$

R control chart:

Centre line   CL = $\bar{R}$ = 25.5
Upper control limit UCL = $D_4\bar{R}$ = 2.115 × 25.5 ≒ 53.9
Lower control limit LCL = $D_3\bar{R}$ (none)

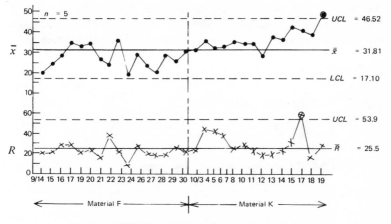

Figure 13.30 Control chart drawn using total data.

Step 7. Make a control chart by writing in small dots and crosses for data values and connecting them with lines.

The width between the upper and lower control limit lines on the $\bar{x}$ control chart is 14.71 × 2 = 29.42 (1/1000 mm). If we assume that the length of one centimetre on the graph paper is equivalent to 10.00 (1/1000 mm), the width of the limit lines will be about 3 cm. The width from zero to the upper control limit line on the $\bar{R}$ control chart is 53.9 (1/1000 mm). Accordingly, assuming that one centimetre on the graph paper is equivalent to 20.0 (1/1000 mm), the width will be 3 cm on the paper. After making the control chart, insert the dates on the lateral axis, and connect dots and crosses on the $\bar{x}$ and $\bar{R}$ lines (see figure 13.30).

Step 8. Add the necessary items.

Write the letters $\bar{x}$ and R on the left side of the control chart and n = 5 on the upper left side. As the materials for September and October are different, this must be indicated as well.

189

b) Control chart stratified material-wise

We know that material 'F' was used for September and material 'K' for October, so we can draw a control chart for each. The number of data stratified in this manner will be 75 each, which is a bit too few to draw a control chart. However, considering the main purpose here is to compare the two, we will prepare the chart anyway. A control chart of $n = 5$ and $k = 15$ can be obtained. Drawing the control chart is the same as set out in the above section. Thus the procedure can be simplified here.

i) Control chart for material 'F'

Step 1. Find the totals of $\bar{x}$ and R in each sub-group (see table 13.12).

Step 2. Find the overall mean, $\bar{\bar{x}}$.

$$\bar{\bar{x}} = \frac{20.0 + 24.8 + \ldots + 25.6}{15} = \frac{413.2}{15} \approx 27.55$$

Step 3. Find the average value of the range, $\bar{R}$.

$$\bar{R} = \frac{18 + 21 + \ldots + 26}{15} = \frac{326}{15} \approx 21.7$$

Step 4. Compute the control limit lines.

$\bar{x}$ **control chart**

$\text{CL} = \bar{\bar{x}} = 27.55$

$$\begin{aligned}
\text{UCL} = \bar{\bar{x}} + A_2\bar{R} &= 27.55 + 0.577 \times 21.7 \\
&\approx 27.55 + 12.52 \\
&= 40.07
\end{aligned}$$

$$\begin{aligned}
\text{LCL} = \bar{\bar{x}} - A_2\bar{R} &= 27.55 - 0.577 \times 21.7 \\
&\approx 27.55 - 12.52 \\
&= 15.03
\end{aligned}$$

R **control chart**

$\text{CL} = \bar{R} = 21.7$

$\text{UCL} = D_4\bar{R} = 2.115 \times 21.7 = 45.9$

LCL (none)

Step 5. Make the control chart (see figure 13.31).

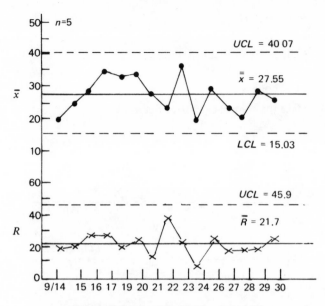

Figure 13.31 Control chart for material F

ii) Control chart for material 'K'

Step 1. Find the total of $\bar{x}$ and R in each sub-group (see table 13.12).

Step 2. Find the overall mean $\bar{\bar{x}}$.

$$\bar{\bar{x}} = \frac{30.8 + 31.2 + \ldots + 47.8}{15} = \frac{541.0}{15} = 36.07$$

Step 3. Find the average value of the range, $\bar{R}$.

$$\bar{R} = \frac{20 + 24 + \ldots + 26}{15} = \frac{438}{15} = 29.2$$

Step 4. Compute the control limit lines.

$\bar{x}$ **control chart**

$$CL = \bar{\bar{x}} = 36.07$$

$$\begin{aligned}
UCL = \bar{\bar{x}} = A_2\bar{R} &= 36.07 + 0.577 \times 29.2 \\
&\approx 36.07 + 16.85 \\
&= 52.92
\end{aligned}$$

$$\begin{aligned}
LCL = \bar{\bar{x}} - A_2\bar{R} &= 36.07 - 0.577 \times 29.2 \\
&\approx 36.07 - 16.85 \\
&= 19.22
\end{aligned}$$

191

R **control chart**

CL = $\bar{R}$ + 29.2

UCL = $D_4\bar{R}$ = 2.115 × 29.2

$\qquad \approx 61.8$

LCL none

Step 5. Make the control chart. (see figure 13.32)

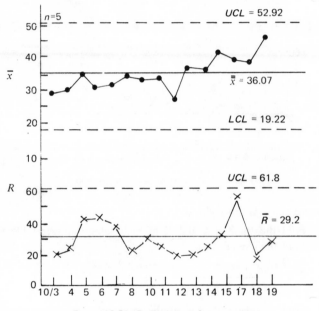

Figure 13.32 Control chart for material K

c) Study

The following information can be obtained by referring to the control charts in figures 13.30, 13.31 and 13.32; with regard to viewing the control chart, refer to chapter 8.

i) Control chart using total data (figure 13.30)

a) One point outside the limits is found in both control chart $\bar{x}$ and control chart R. A run of eight is found in the $\bar{x}$ control chart (between September 24 and October 4) with a trend to rise day by day. This indicated an abnormality in the production process.

b) The control chart line of $\bar{x}$ during September (material F) has four points out of 15 on the upper side of the centre line. In contrast to that, 13 points out of the 15 are found on the upper side of the centre line during October (material K). This indicates a difference of mean values in the production process.

In control chart R, the same trend can be observed during October (material K), but the difference is not as great as in control chart $\bar{x}$. From the above results, it is necessary to stratify September data (material F) and October data (material K) respectively, and compose the control data charts.

ii) Stratified control charts (figure 13.31 and 13.32)

c) As was clearly observed in figures 13.31 and 13.32, $\bar{\bar{x}}$ and $\bar{R}$ for October (material K) are higher in both $\bar{x}$ and R control charts than the ones for September (material F). In particular, the $\bar{\bar{x}}$ values show a large difference in the two $\bar{x}$ control charts.

d) The control charts show an almost well-controlled condition in September (material F) and it is considered that the production process was normal during that month.

e) As $\bar{R}$ is high for October (material K), the point outside the UCL in figure 13.30 is now within it. As $\bar{\bar{x}}$ is high compared with September (material F), the point outside the UCL is also within the limit. However, $\bar{x}$ during October, with a run of nine points followed by a run of six points, showed a clear tendency to rise.

iii) Summary

a) There is a significant difference between the data collected in September (material F) and October (material K). October (material K) has a higher mean value, but at the present stage it is not evident that the cause is due to either material or change of month.

b) The $\bar{x}$ control chart shows a rising trend day by day in the October (material K) control chart. It cannot be determined if this cause is due to a fault in the material itself, lowered precision of the machine tools, or environmental conditions. Consequently, it is important to make a study of these matters on a technical basis.

13.8 Control charts II

The following experiment was carried out to study the changes shown by points plotted on a *p* control chart.

First, 1,000 small beads were placed in an appropriate container. There were 150 green ones (15 per cent), 200 yellow ones (20 per cent), and 70 red ones (7 per cent); the rest were white.

a) A random sampling of 50 beads was taken from the container and the number of green beads in the sample was counted. The 50 beads were put back in the container and the same process was repeated 25 times. The results are shown in table 13.13. The results of this experiment are equivalent to the data on defectives from a production process where the average fraction defective is 15 per cent.

b) A random sampling of 50 beads was taken from the container and this time the number of yellow beads was counted. When this was repeated ten times, the data shown in table 13.14 was obtained. This time the results are equivalent to the data where the average fraction defective is 20 per cent.

c) The same thing was repeated ten times for the red beads. The data obtained are given in table 13.15. This data is equivalent to an average fraction defective of 7 per cent.

Make a *p* control chart using the data in table 13.13. (The value for *n* is given, so a *pn* control chart can also be made. But, in this case, only make a *p* chart.)

Extend the limit line of the chart you have just drawn and mark dots for the data of the fraction defective in tables 13.14 and 13.15.

This chart shows that the initial fraction defective, which was 15 per cent, changed to 20 per cent, and then to 7 per cent. Now, examine to what extent the changes in the production process were reflected in changes in the control chart.

Table 13.13

Sub-group No.	Size of sampling (sub-group size)	No. of green beads (defectives)	Sub-group No.	Size of sampling (sub-group size)	No. of green beads (defectives)
1	50	9	14	50	9
2	"	8	15	"	7
3	"	12	16	"	3
4	"	6	17	"	8
5	"	8	18	"	3
6	"	8	19	"	5
7	"	10	20	"	4
8	"	13	21	"	10
9	"	9	22	"	10
10	"	5	23	"	9
11	"	13	24	"	4
12	"	3	25	"	6
13	"	5			

Table 13.14

Table 13.15

Sub-group No.	Size of sampling (sub-group size)	No. of yellow beads (defectives)	Sub-group No.	Size of sampling (sub-group size)	No. of red beads (defectives)
26	50	9	36	50	5
27	"	14	37	"	3
28	"	12	38	"	6
29	"	7	39	"	1
30	"	10	40	"	3
31	"	6	41	"	7
32	"	17	42	"	4
33	"	11	43	"	6
34	"	12	44	"	3
35	"	8	45	"	4

This is an exercise to determine how the points on a *p* chart move when the fraction defective of the production process is changed. Let's make the control chart according to the procedures described in chapter 8.

a) Green beads control chart

Step 1. Determine the fraction defective, p, in each sub-group. For instance, in the initial sub-group, $p = 9/50 = 0.18$.

Also, determine p in subsequent sub-groups and mark them down on the data sheet (see table 13.13A).

Step 2. Obtain the average fraction defective,

$$\bar{p} = \frac{187}{1250} = 0.1496 \fallingdotseq 0.150$$

Green beads

Table 13.13A

Sub-group No.	Sub-group size (n)	No. of defectives (pn)	Fraction defective (p)	Sub-group No.	Sub-group size (n)	No. of defectives (pn)	Fraction defective (p)
1	50	9	0.18	14	50	9	0.18
2	''	8	0.16	15	''	7	0.14
3	''	12	0.24	16	''	3	0.06
4	''	6	0.12	17	''	8	0.16
5	''	8	0.16	18	''	3	0.06
6	''	8	0.16	19	''	5	0.10
7	''	10	0.20	20	''	4	0.08
8	''	13	0.26	21	''	10	0.20
9	''	9	0.18	22	''	10	0.20
10	''	5	0.10	23	''	9	0.18
11	''	13	0.26	24	''	4	0.08
12	''	3	0.06	25	''	6	0.12
13	''	5	0.10	Total	1250	187	—

Yellow beads

Table 13.14A

Sub-group No.	Sub-group size (n)	No. of defectives (pn)	Fraction defective (p)
26	50	9	0.18
27	''	14	0.28
28	''	12	0.24
29	''	7	0.14
30	''	10	0.20
31	''	6	0.12
32	''	17	0.34
33	''	11	0.22
34	''	12	0.24
35	''	8	0.16

Red beads

Table 13.15A

Sub-group No.	Sub-group size (n)	No. of defectives (pn)	Fraction defective (p)
36	50	5	0.10
37	''	3	0.06
38	''	6	0.12
39	''	1	0.02
40	''	3	0.06
41	''	7	0.14
42	''	4	0.08
43	''	6	0.12
44	''	3	0.06
45	''	4	0.08

Step 3. Determine the control limits.

Centre line: $\qquad$ CL = $\bar{p}$ = 0.150

Upper control limit: UCL = $\bar{p} + 3\sqrt{\dfrac{\bar{p}(1 - \bar{p})}{n}}$

$$= 0.150 + 0.42 \times 0.357$$
$$\doteqdot 0.150 + 0.150$$
$$= 0.300$$

Lower control limit: LCL = $\bar{p} - 3\sqrt{\dfrac{\bar{p}(1 - \bar{p})}{n}}$

$$\doteqdot 0.150 - 0.150$$
$$= 0$$

Step 4. Make the control lines and plot p (see figure 13.33).

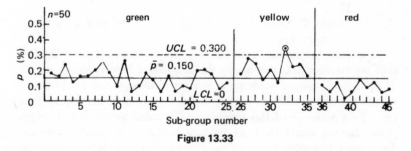

Figure 13.33

As is obvious from the exercise, the green bead points form a control chart for a process where the fraction defective is constant at 15 per cent. Even when the fraction defective is constant, it is apparent that points on the chart show dispersion. However, when the fraction defective is fixed during the production process, there are no points outside the control line and the position of the points will not assume a particular shape. In other words, this constitutes a controlled state.

b) Yellow beads control chart

Step 1. Determine the fraction defective in each sub-group (see table 13.14).

Step 2. Extend the control chart for the green beads and plot the point p (see figure 13.33).

197

As a result, the data of sub-group number 32 is outside the upper control limit. At the same time, although the position of the points is not in apparent disorder, we can observe that on the whole they tend to rise towards the upper limit.

The control chart shown in figure 13.33 is similar to one where the fraction defective is changed from 15 per cent to 20 per cent. The variations in the production process can be observed from the existence of a point outside the limit line of the chart and showing undesirable tendencies. However, the extent of the change in this case is not so large, and the abnormality is not noticeable at the points between sub-groups 26 to 31. Consequently, there is some risk of not noticing the change in the production process. To modify the control chart so that any slight change can be quickly observed, enlarge n and narrow the width of both the upper and lower control lines.

c) Red beads control chart

Step 1. Determine the fraction defective of p in each sub-group (see table 13.15).

Step 2. Extend the control chart for green beads and plot the points p (see figure 13.33).

As a result, all the points on the chart are located below $\bar{p}$, indicating that the fraction defective during the production process has decreased. The points for the red beads are equivalent to the case where the fraction defective in the production process is improved from 15 per cent to 7 per cent. Even a change of this magnitude is revealed by the points on the chart, showing that there is an apparent change in the process situation. This makes it possible to have a better grasp of changes in the production process.

Experimenting with beads to study the trends of points on the control chart, as we have done here, is an excellent way of determining the effectiveness of the control chart.

The beads that have been used in these experiments can be purchased from the Japan Standards Association. Further studies, based on various situations, should be carried out in the same way.

13.9 Scatter diagrams

During certain production processes, it is necessary to decrease the moisture content of intermediate products. Thus the problem was the moisture content in the raw material.

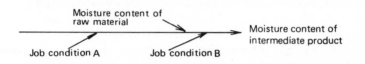

The data shown below represent the percentages of moisture content of the raw material (*x*) and moisture content of the intermediate product (*y*) made from it (unit: per cent). *x* and *y* form a pair of corresponding data.

Question:

1 Study the procedures from the analysis of the present state and how to control the process.

2 Assuming that the *y* value is to be kept below 1.8%, determine the *x* value to be controlled. In this case, there are two kinds of instruments, A and B, for measuring *y*. When measuring with instrument B, the bias is about plus 0.4% as compared with A. (▲ mark in the table indicates measurements with instrument B).

No.	x	y	No.	x	y	No.	x	y	No.	x	y
1	1.10	1.40	14	1.85	2.10▲	27	1.35	1.70	39	1.80	1.70
2	1.25	1.70	15	1.40	2.00▲	28	1.15	2.00▲	40	1.35	1.80▲
3	1.05	1.85▲	16	1.50	1.50	29	1.05	1.85▲	41	1.65	1.55
4	1.60	2.05▲	17	1.60	2.30▲	30	1.20	1.40	42	1.05	1.70▲
5	1.05	1.30	18	1.80	1.90	31	1.35	2.10▲	43	1.30	1.50
6	1.55	2.30▲	19	1.10	1.60▲	32	1.00	1.35	44	1.30	2.30▲
7	1.75	1.75	20	1.60	1.75▲	33	1.60	2.10▲	45	1.45	1.55
8	1.40	2.00▲	21	1.85	2.40▲	34	1.40	1.30	46	1.20	1.55
9	1.30	1.30	22	1.70	2.30▲	35	1.60	1.60	47	1.45	1.80▲
10	1.30	1.90▲	23	1.50	1.40	36	1.50	1.85	48	1.90	1.90
11	1.15	1.20	24	1.40	1.50	37	1.45	2.20▲	49	1.30	1.70▲
12	1.70	1.40	25	1.55	1.90▲	38	1.20	1.80▲	50	1.65	1.70
13	1.60	1.95	26	1.45	2.15▲						

a) Steps to study for standardization

We assume that you have been taught at the QC circle about the following procedures for improvement of quality control:

i) Discover what the problem is (Pareto diagram of cause-and-effect data)

ii) Discover the possible causes of problems (cause-and-effect diagram)

iii) Determine the weight of causes (Pareto diagram)

iv) Study the countermeasures (apply the JM method, etc)

v) Take action (keep close check on the schedule of action)

vi) Study the results (repeat i to v if necessary)

vii) Maintain the controlled state (determination or improvement/abolition of the control points and standard)

When reviewing the problems presented here, following these procedures, points (i) to (iii) have already been carried out and we are at stage (iv) where countermeasures have to be planned. In terms of this specific problem, this means: "Let's decrease the moisture content of the intermediate product by reducing the moisture content of the raw materials."

Given the limited space here, let's concentrate on the study of the problem. The fact that "when measuring the moisture content of the intermediate product with measuring instrument B a bias of plus 0.4% is produced" can be determined naturally from the control data of the measuring instrument itself, or a graph of the moisture content percentage in the intermediate product. If graph y is modified and compared with graph x, the information needed can be obtained as is described in the following practice problem on a binomial probability paper. In other words, even if the data are not gathered for a specific purpose, study and analysis can be carried out with the ordinary stratified control graphs.

Since we are studying analysis by means of a scatter diagram (which is comparatively easy to make and can be read at a glance), let's continue with our study according to the following procedure:

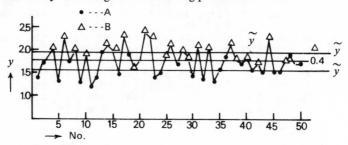

Figure 13.34 Moisture content percentage of an intermediate product

Table 13.16

	●	△	(Total)
Above the limit	4	21	25
Below the limit	21	4	25
(Total)	25	25	50

Note: The moisture content percentages may differ significantly according to whether measuring instrument A or B is used.

1 Make a scatter diagram.
2 Study the scatter diagram and stratification.
3 Make a scatter diagram with corrected data.
4 Make a significant test of correlation.
5 Find the relationship between x and y.
6 Obtain the limit line of x so as to keep the y value below 1.8%.
7 Determine the means of keeping the x value within the limit.
8 Take action by the method determined in 7 (above).
9 Check the results.
10 Standardize the results.

b) Obtaining x to keep the y value below 1.8%

Step 1. Make a scatter diagram

Plot the data from No. 1 to No. 50, using the vertical axis for x and the horizontal axis for y. The data for y values obtained with measuring instrument A are plotted as solid black circles (●), and with B as triangles (△) (figure 13.35).

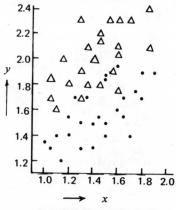

Figure 13.35 Scatter diagram

201

Step 2. Study the scatter diagram and stratification

When viewing figure 13.35 as a whole, there seems to be no correlation. However, there does seem to be a correlation if the data are stratified by the two measuring instruments A and B.

Step 3. Make a scatter diagram with corrected data

In this problem, y data measured with instrument B resulted in about a plus 0.4% bias. Lower the plots with (△) mark by 0.4 along the longitudinal axis (subtract 0.4 from each y value of the plots) and re-plot them so they will be rearranged as in figure 13.36.

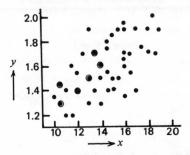

Figure 13.36 Scatter diagram using corrected data

Step 4. Significant test for correlation

When we look at figure 13.36, it seems to show correlation. Put down $\tilde{x}$ and $\tilde{y}$ on the diagram according to the procedure explained in chapter 9, and count the number of points in each area (figure 13.37).

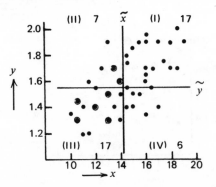

Figure 13.37 Inspecting for correlation using a median line

The total number of points on figure 13.37 is 34 in areas I and III, 13 for areas II and IV, and the number on the median line is 3. When referring to table 9.5 in chapter 9, we find there is a significant positive correlation between them.

Step 5.   *Obtaining the relationship between x and y*

Assume that we have found a positive correlation between x and y, how can this relationship be presented? There are two forms assumed by positive correlation: When the points in one of the two diagrams showing degree of correlation are scattered and in the other are concentrated as shown in figure 13.38, and when the degree of change in y against x, that is the gradient, is different as shown in the two diagrams in figure 13.39. The former is represented by a coefficient of correlation as mentioned in chapter 9. In contrast, the latter is shown by the regression line (regression line equation) which is being introduced here for the first time. (There is a difference of correlation coefficient even in the latter, and the graph on the left in figure 13.39 has a stronger correlation than the one on the right.)

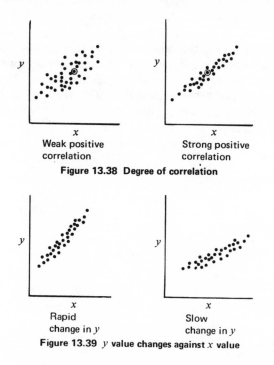

Weak positive
correlation

Strong positive
correlation

Figure 13.38   Degree of correlation

Rapid
change in y

Slow
change in y

Figure 13.39 y value changes against x value

As for points on the right of $\widetilde{x}$ in figure 13.40, obtain $\widetilde{x}_R$ and $\widetilde{y}_R$ on the graph and make their point of intersection R. As for plots on the left of the $\widetilde{x}$ axis, obtain $\widetilde{x}_L$ and $\widetilde{y}_L$ and make their point of intersection L. Then, connect R and L with a line. This R-L line is a *regression line* representing the relationship between x and y.

> *Note:* The regression line expressing the relationship between x and y can be given as a regression line equation calculated from the data.

Step 6. *Obtaining the limit of x with the regression line*

According to the arrangement shown in figure 13.41 (marked with arrow), the x value which corresponds to $y = 1.8$ will be 1.7. In other words, to control the y values so as to keep them below 1.8 per cent, it will be sufficient if value x is kept below 1.7 per cent.

> *Note:* As can be seen from the figure, even when the x value is 1.6, y values are dispersed between 1.35 and 1.95. In practice, therefore, a more accurate limit value of x should be determined considering such things as dispersion, economy and inspection. In discussing the limits of the x value, the problem here has been simplified for a clearer explanation.

Step 7. With regard to the items subsequent to procedure 7 discussed in the general procedures, they are used not only for analysis and improvement by means of the scatter diagram; they are commonly used for other purposes as well. They do not represent the method itself, but the general concept, so I will not go into a description here.

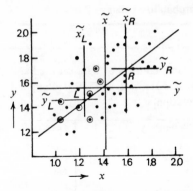

Figure 13.40 Obtaining the regression line

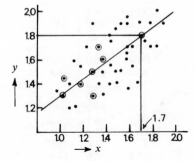

Figure 13.41 Obtaining the limit value of x

205

13.10 Binomial probability paper

The following table consists of data on the hardness of three shades of lipstick (Nos. 501, 502 and 503) compiled during the initial month of production.

No.	Batch 1				Batch 2			
	Lip-stick No.	Raw material lot No.	Temp.	Hard-ness	Lip-stick No.	Raw material lot No.	Temp.	Hard-ness
1	501	A	72.8	22.7	501	A	72.5	22.9
2	''	''	73.1	23.3	''	''	72.8	23.2
3	502	''	74.2	24.6	502	''	72.9	24.9
4	''	''	71.5	22.9	''	''	72.4	24.0
5	''	''	73.2	23.5	''	''	72.1	23.4
6	''	''	74.2	23.9	''	''	73.5	24.3
7	503	''	73.4	24.8	503	''	73.8	25.7
8	''	''	72.2	24.9	''	''	72.0	24.2
9	''	''	72.5	24.7	501	''	72.6	22.8
10	501	''	73.4	23.3	502	''	73.7	24.3
11	502	''	74.5	24.6	503	''	72.2	24.8
12	501	''	72.3	23.6	''	''	73.5	24.9
13	503	''	72.4	25.0	''	''	73.8	25.3
14	''	''	73.4	25.5	502	''	74.1	24.4
15	502	''	72.3	23.6	''	B	72.5	24.1
16	503	B	74.1	26.9	503	''	72.2	26.6
17	501	''	71.9	24.9	501	''	72.8	24.9
18	''	''	73.7	26.2	''	''	72.4	24.4
19	''	''	72.5	24.7	502	''	73.9	25.2
20	502	''	72.2	24.6	501	''	74.3	25.3
21	503	''	74.5	27.6	503	''	72.3	25.6
22	''	''	71.9	26.8	501	''	73.1	26.5
23	501	''	73.5	26.2	502	''	72.4	24.9
24	502	''	73.8	25.3	''	''	74.5	26.2
25	503	''	74.3	26.8	501	''	73.6	26.4

Production is being carried out in the form of two batches every day, batch 1 and batch 2. There is a very close relationship between the hardness of the lipstick and the raw material. The lot of this material is changed in the middle of the month from A lot to B lot. The B lot was accepted close to the upper limit of the specification. Thus the inspection section wishes to have information about the performance of the B lot. The temperature when the lipstick is poured is considered to have an effect on the hardness. In this case, production was carried out at the standardized temperature of $73°C \pm 2°C$ because of processing conditions.

Process capability analysis can be made based on this information to determine a method for process control for the subsequent months. Carry out the process analysis by means of a simple test with a binomial probability paper.

This exercise is to carry out an analysis by a very simple method which, by stratifying the production batch, shade and material lot, can help us determine whether there is any distinction among them and also whether, by expressing data in graph form, there is a correlation between hardness and the temperature when pouring. Then let us work out appropriate action on the basis of the results of the analysis and our technical evaluation.

a) Making the graph and testing for differences in stratified factors

First we must determine the marks to be used to indicate the data in order to identify the stratified factors. In this case, the symbols used are given in table 13.17 and they have been used to prepare the graph shown in figure 13.42. Draw a horizontal line (median line) on the graph dividing the points into approximately even numbers. Next, the usual procedure is to count the number of plotted points found above and below the median line with regard to the stratified factors. But, in this case, it was decided that the primary step would be to inspect the influence of known abnormal lots of raw material. In other words, count the number of points found above and below the median line with regard to material lots A and B (table 13.18). Make a 2 x 2 contingency table as shown in figure 13.43. When testing the contingency table by means of the R range as shown in figure 13.43, it will be found to have a high level of significance as the short distance is longer than the length of one per cent of the $N = 2$ R scale.

Table 13.17

No.	501	502	503
Batch 1	○	□	△
Batch 2	●	■	▲

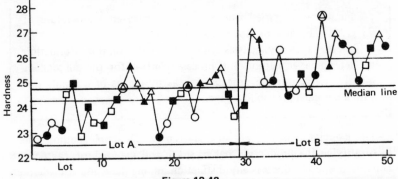

Figure 13.42

Table 13.18

	Material lot A	Material lot B	Total
Above median	7	17	24
Below median	20	4	24
Total	27	21	48

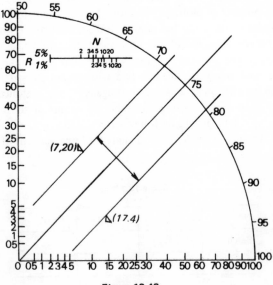

Figure 13.43

The B lot material is obviously different from the normal A lot. The hardness standard of lipstick is 24 ± 3 and among the lipsticks made from lot B we can find one sample that does not meet the hardness standard. Fortunately, material of normal lots could be obtained. Therefore, it was decided that material B should be mixed with the normal lots for further production.

When there is a substantial difference between the materials, it is hard to see the difference between other stratified factors. Thus we will try to adjust the graph for this purpose. Figure 13.44 shows the graph with the median lines drawn for both lots A and B and where lot B is corrected to the level of lot A.

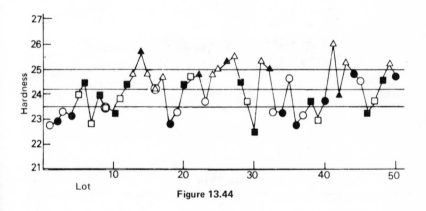

Figure 13.44

Tables 13.19 and 13.20 are obtained by making the contingency table for batch and shade respectively in the same way as was done for the materials. With regard to table 13.18, even without further test, it is clear that there is no difference between the two groups. As concerns colour stratification, there is a high level of significance as shown in figure 13.45 where the difference is obvious. The hardness of No. 503 is different from that of the others. When 501 and 502 are tested separately from 503, there is no significant difference. We can control the production process of 503 by using a separate chart, and 501 and 502 by combining them in one chart.

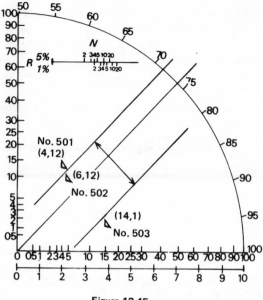

Figure 13.45

Table 13.19

	Batch 1	Batch 2	Total
Above median	12	12	24
Below median	13	12	25
Total	25	24	49

Table 13.20

	501	502	503	Total
Above median	4	6	14	24
Below median	12	12	1	25
Total	16	18	15	49

Finally, let us analyze the relationship between the temperature when pouring and the hardness. To observe the correlation between hardness and temperature, we must make a graph in which differences in terms of shade are not considered. In the graph for hardness, figure 13.46, a correction has been made for differences in hardness in 503, 502 and 501. Hardness will then be represented by x and temperature by y.

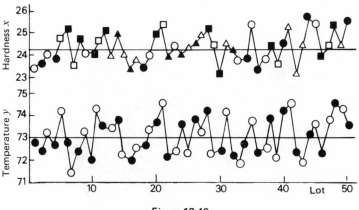

Figure 13.46

If we use the method of determining correlation by means of whether points are above or below the median, we find that $n_+ = 40$ and $n_- = 10$ (**'B'**) Also, using the method in which the direction of lines connecting plotted values is the basis, $n_+ = 36$ and $n_- = 12$ (**'A'**). Thus, as shown in figure 13.47, it has a high level of significance. The coefficient of correlation r is 0.81 for **'B'** and 0.68 for **'A'**, while the coefficient of contribution r^2 is 0.65 in the case of **'B'** and 0.47 in the case of **'A'**.

B' Correlation using the median $n_+ = 40$ $n_- = 10$

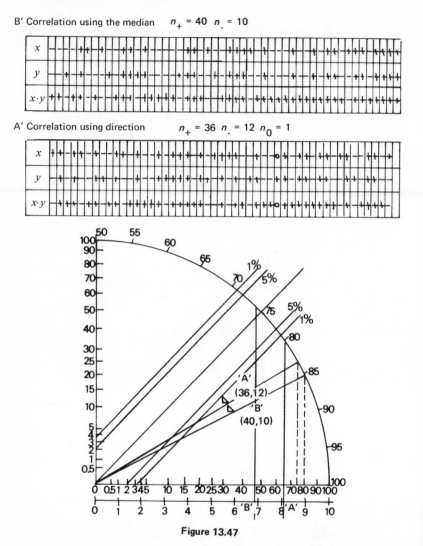

A' Correlation using direction $n_+ = 36$ $n_- = 12$ $n_0 = 1$

Figure 13.47

As expected, we have proven that the pouring temperature is closely correlated to the hardness. By making a thorough analysis of the hardness graph, the correlation to temperature could also be proven. We could not have attained such a result from the first graph (figure 13.42) alone. The range of temperature for pouring the molten lipstick was within the standards and the hardness of the product was normal. Thus production control can be carried out under the same standards.

13.11 Sampling

---

(1) There are various principles to be considered for correct sampling. Give more than three principles and the reasons for each.

a) Clarify the purpose and action

The purpose for investigating the characteristics of lots through sampling methods should always be clear. The property to be measured may be composition, moisture content, size distribution, etc and the sampling methods, treatment of the samples, speed of sampling, and subsequent action will differ according to each particular characteristic.

The action that will have to be taken, based on the data obtained by measurements, should be made clear in advance.

There are basically two different grounds for collecting data: those related to lots, such as inspection; and those related to production processes, such as process control and analysis.

b) Stratification

Determine what the lot is to be, that is, study thoroughly how sampling should be carried out, while considering the population.

If the sampling error is large, wrong action may be taken. So we must know how to select the lot taking stratification into consideration if we are to correctly estimate the lot characteristics. For example, rather than merely consider a purchased lot, we can carry out further stratification according to the manufacturer, manufacturing machines, or the time of manufacture. And, by considering any dispersions in the sub-lots, we may increase precision and reduce costs. A rather effective method in sampling is to take past data (control limits of the control chart or dispersion of the sub-lots) into consideration, or control dispersion in advance by means of experimentation. In either case, we see how important it is to consider stratification first of all.

c) Random sampling

In sampling, the parameters of a lot (mean value or dispersion) can be estimated by measuring the size of sample. Thus any bias or precision in the estimates should be reduced to a minimum. For this purpose, all parts of the lot must be given the same chance to appear in the samples. In other words, random sampling is essential. There are various methods of making

213

random sampling, so it is important to adopt the most appropriate one in keeping with the properties studied and the working conditions.

d) Caution on sampling errors

All the points set forth in the paragraphs on stratification and random sampling must be applied in order to avoid any sampling errors.

Moreover, it is important to keep the sampling work in a controlled state. For the sampling to be precise, it is indispensable to control the sources of error by analyzing the various causes and standardizing them, by carrying out maintenance of the sampling instruments and training personnel.

e) Establishing sampling methods

Sampling must be accomplished taking into account all technical and economic conditions. Random sampling is not always suitable. If we select samples from, say, the end of a coiled product (steel or paper), we do so for the sake of economy. It is therefore necessary to select significant samples to control and evaluate to what extent the sampling method includes a bias between the end and the whole coil.

Note: The following exercise, (2), shows how to carry out sampling when receiving a consignment of imported iron ore to determine whether to accept or reject it. This exercise can be applied to other mineral products such as coal, cement and so on. The general rules for sampling powder and lump ore such as mineral products are specified in Japan Industrial Standard M8100 and ISO Standard IS 3081.

---

(2) As shown in the drawing below, the material is being moved towards the production process. How do you think it should be sampled?

The iron ore is unloaded from the ore carrier, moved along a belt conveyor, and stacked in the yard. What is the best method for obtaining samples to analyze the substance?

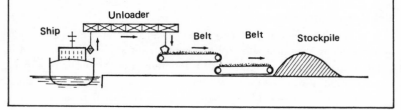

---

a) Sampling procedure

The procedure for sampling and sample preparation is roughly as follows:

i) Determine which lot is to be sampled.

ii) Take random sampling from the required number of increments (unit volume of powder and lump ore that are sampled from the lot or sub-lot).

iii) Collect the increments for gross samples.

iv) If necessary, prepare the sample to be tested by crushing or condensing the gross sample. An example of this is given in figure 13.48.

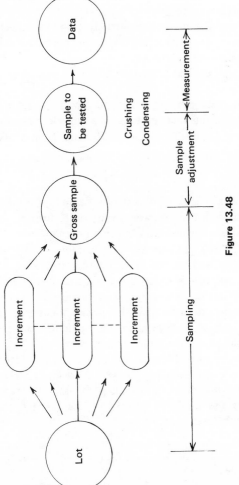

Figure 13.48

b) Types of sampling

There are four types of sampling depending on the form of lot, transportation method, and method of taking increments.

i) Belt Sampling: When lots are moved by conveyor belt, increments can be sampled directly from the belt or the end of the belt.

ii) Hatch Sampling: This is a method of sampling increments from the hatches during loading or unloading when the lots are transferred.

iii) Wagon Sampling: This method is used when lots are delivered by truck or car, but it is not applicable in the case of this practice problem.

iv) Vessel Sampling: This method is used when lots are delivered in sacks, drums or other vessels but again it is not applicable for this practice problem.

When a conveyor belt is used for loading or unloading, the belt method is recommended because:

— As a rule, sampling is performed while the lot is moving.

— Increments must be taken at a time close to weighing of the lot.

— It is impossible to take increments from a pile of samples at random.

c) Size of lot

The lot size should be determined for the following purposes:

i) To determine the mean quality of the lot.

ii) To take the necessary action for each lot.

In this case, the aim is to know the contents of the raw material that has been delivered. Thus one ship should be taken as equivalent to one lot if the raw material is essentially the same. It is usually advisable to compose the lots so that they are as homogeneous as possible. When inspecting a lot to determine the price, bonuses or penalties, on a commercial basis, it is necessary for the producer and user to determine the criteria and procedures by prior agreement.

To determine suoh points, it is necessary to consider matters such as past experience and technical knowhow, facilities and process requirements of the user, cost of sampling and sample preparation, process capability of the producer, history of the lot and the difficulty or precision of sampling.

d) Size and number of increments

After the lot size has been decided upon, the size and number of the increments must be determined. The larger the size of the increments, the less the dispersion of the characteristic values among the increments. This relationship shows an asymptote, so higher precision can be obtained by increasing the number of increments rather than by increasing their size. Moreover, since we want the size of the increment to be five to 10 times larger than the maximum lump size of the lot, the size of the increment must be determined by means of the maximum lump size of the ore.

Next, the number of increments must be determined to satisfy fully the required precision of each characteristic of the lot according to its size, quality and dispersion.

e) Belt sampling

With this method, sampling is carried out by taking samples from the moving belt conveyor. The intervals between the samples taken must be determined in advance so that the prescribed number of increments can be sampled from the entire lot. Systematic sampling is more precise than random sampling, and is easier to follow as a work standard for sampling instruction and automation. In this case, observe the following points.

i) Random start. Determine where (when) to take the initial increment at random.

ii) Determine the interval between samples, taking into account ore not being conveyed on the belt at a regular interval.

iii) Note carefully the periodicity of the lot being conveyed on the belt.

iv) Since the distribution of grain-size material on the right and left side and the upper and lower portion of the material carried by the belt differs, take out the designated amount at the full width and at all depths of the belt-carried material.

f) Automatic sampler

The automatic sampler is a highly effective means of rapid and accurate belt sampling. This sampler generally employs a chute on the conveyor. When using this device, note the following items.

i) Carry out investigations and experiments in advance to obtain the most effective use.

ii) Strive for high reliability (obtain easy cleaning, avoid mechanical faults and bias).

iii) The increment size and sampling interval must be flexible.

217

g) How to gather the increments

When sampling increments from a lot, either get samples to be tested from each increment (figure 13.49), or gather all increments for gross sampling (figure 13.50).

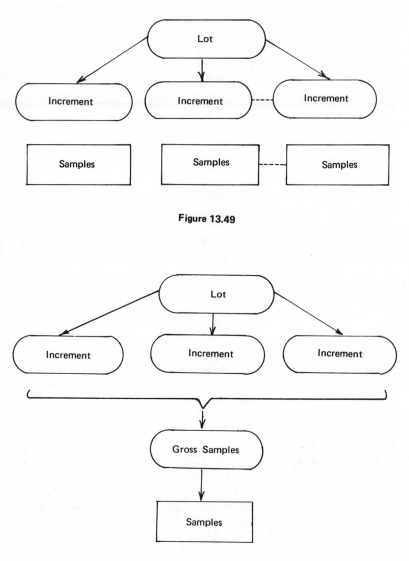

Figure 13.49

Figure 13.50

13.12 Sampling inspection

(1) When $p_0 = 2.5\%$, $\alpha \approx 0.05$, $p_1 = 15\%$ and $\beta \approx 0.10$ are given, obtain a single sampling inspection plan (n, c) by attributes.

$p_0 = 2.5\%$, $p_1 = 15\%$, $\alpha \approx 0.05$, $\beta \approx 0.10$

Employ the Table of Standard Single Sampling Inspection by Attributes ($\alpha \approx 0.05$, $\beta \approx 0.10$) on page 127 (table 12.4). (Table 13.21 is abbreviated.)

Step 1. A column where $p_1 = 15(\%)$ is included is in the horizontal column, for $p_1(\%)$ values of 14.1 to 18.0.

Step 2. A column where $p_0 = 2.5(\%)$ is included is in the vertical column, for $p_0(\%)$ values of 2.25 to 2.80.

Step 3. At the intersection of these two columns, the n is equal to 30 and c is equal to 2. Consequently, $n = 30$ and $c = 2$.

Table 13.21

p_1 (%) p_0 (%)	0.71 0.90		14.1 18.0
0.090 0.112			
2.25 2.80	·········	·········→	30 2

(2) Adapting a single sampling inspection based on MIL-STD-105D tables, and AQL = 1.2%, lot size of 3,700 and inspection level II designated in purchasing inspection, prepare three kinds of sampling inspection plans such as normal inspection, tightened inspection and reduced inspection. Hint: As AQL = 1.2(%) is not shown in the tables, employ the AQL = 1.5(%)

Since we are given: AQL = 1.2(%), N = 3,700, inspection level II and a single sampling inspection, the procedure is as follows.

Step 1. Find the correct sample code letter in the column of normal inspection level II, with N = 3,700, in MIL Table I (table 12.6 on page 130). It is sample code L.

Step 2. The acceptance number, Ac, rejection number, Re, and sample size, n, can be obtained by using MIL Table II-A (table 12.7 on page 131) and the columns AQL and sample code L in normal inspection of a single sampling plan. As 1.2% is not shown in the AQL column, use the AQL = 1.5(%) column. Then n = 200, Ac = 7, Re = 8 can be obtained.

Step 3. Obtain the sample size of n, acceptance number Ac and rejection number Re, using Table II-B (table 12.8) in tightened inspection of a single sampling plan in the same manner as that of step 1 and 2. As a result, n = 200, Ac = 5 and Re = 6.

Step 4. Obtain n, Ac and Re using Table II-C (table 12.9 on page 133) in reduced inspection of a single sampling plan in the same way as described in steps 1 and 2. Then n = 80, Ac = 3, and Re = 6 can be obtained.

The values obtained are arranged in table 13.22.

Table 13.22

	Normal inspection	Tightened inspection	Reduced inspection
sample size, n	200	200	80
Number of accepted, Ac	7	5	3
Number rejected, Re	8	6	6

(3) Assuming that $N = 1,000$, $p_0 = 2.5\%$ and $p_1 = 10\%$ ($\alpha \approx 0.05$ and $\beta \approx 0.10$) obtain sampling inspection plans (n, c), and when undertaking equivalent sampling inspection according to MIL-STD-105D, what is the AQL? Hint: Get n and c from the Table of Standard Single Sampling Inspection by Attributes. When $N = 1,000$ and inspection level is II, compare n to Ac, Re of the MIL-STD-105D single sampling inspection tables to find the AQL. What are some of the things that can be discovered from these comparisons?

Under the conditions where $N = 1,000$, $p_0 = 2.5(\%)$, $p_1 = 10(\%)$, $\alpha \approx 0.05$ and $\beta \approx 0.10$, first find the sample size of n and acceptance number of c from table 12.4. We find that the columns that satisfy the conditions $p_0 = 2.5(\%)$, $p_1 = 10(\%)$, $\alpha \approx 0.05$ and $\beta \approx 0.10$, indicate $n = 70$ and $c = 4$.

Next, to obtain the sample size code letter at inspection level II, $N = 1,000$, we use table 12.6 and find that the letter is J.

From table 12.7, we find that $n = 80$ when the sample size code letter is J. Moreover, the relationship between the AQL column and Ac, Re is as follows.

AQL   1.0(%) $Ac = 2$, $Re = 3$
AQL   1.5(%) $Ac = 3$, $Re = 4$
AQL   2.5(%) $Ac = 5$, $Re = 6$

Let's not make difficult calculations here. Instead, we can compare our findings from tables 12.4, 12.6 and 12.7. It is found that the value of the AQL closest to $p_0 = 2.5(\%)$ (table 12.4) is within the $1.5 \sim 2.5(\%)$ range (table 12.7, after using table 12.6). However, while the representative values of AQL are 1.5(%) and 2.5(%), the latter seems to be most appropriate. In other words, the acceptance number of fraction defective is almost identical.

Appendix I: Sign Test Table

(1) Definition

Let us assume a sample is given that is composed of measurements, each of which has plus or minus signs. The sign test table is the table by which to test whether this sample was drawn from a population that has an equal number of plus values and minus values.

(2) Characteristics

Let n denote the sample size and r denote the number of occurrences of either sign, then the distribution of r will be the binomial distribution with a population probability of 0.5, provided the sample is randomly drawn.

Since the distribution is symmetric, $n-r$ may be used instead of r.

In other words, this gives the upper and the lower limits for r of a sample from populations having a fraction defective of 50 per cent at the specified level of significance (or risk) on both sides.

(3) Composition of the table

The left column shows the sample size n and Pr denotes the significance level in relation to the upper and lower limits. The numbers of occurrence r of either sign are given in the corresponding spaces.

When n becomes larger than 90, use $[(n - 1)/2 - k \sqrt{n + 1}\,]$ as an approximation of r, where $[\;]$ denotes the Gauss' notation which indicates the nearest integer below the contents of itself $[\;]$, where k is, respectively, 1.2879, 0.9800, 0.0627 and 0.0123 for the significance level of 1%, 5%, 95% and 99%.

(4) Examples

(a) If n is equal to 60 and the number of plus signs or minus signs is 19 or less or 41 or more, it is significant at 1% risk while not significant when both of them are between 20 and 40.

(b) Significance test of correlation

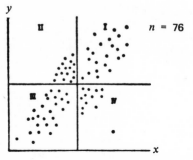

In the scatter diagram, draw median lines parallel to the y-axis and x-axis respectively. The scattered points fall into one of four areas. Give a plus sign to the points in areas I and III and a minus sign to those in areas II and IV. The numbers of the points in the four areas when $n = 76$ are as follows:

$$
\begin{aligned}
\text{I + III} &\ \ldots\ldots\ldots\ldots\ldots\ldots\ \ 22 + 26 = 48 \\
\text{II + IV} &\ \ldots\ldots\ldots\ldots\ldots\ldots\ \ 16 + 12 = 28 \\
\hline
n &\hspace{5.5cm} 76
\end{aligned}
$$

(If n, total number of points, is odd, the median lines are drawn through the point in the centre.)

If there is no correlation, the occurrence ratios of (I + III) and (II + IV) should be 50% each. In the row of $n = 76$, and in the column of 5% of the table, the upper limit of 48, the lower limit of 28, which are equal to I + III = 48, II + IV = 28, are shown. Thus it can be said that the correlation exists. Moreover, since (I + III) $>$ (II + IV), the correlation is positive.

Sign Test Table

n	Lower limit 1%	Lower limit 5%	Upper limit 5%	Upper limit 1%	n	Lower limit 1%	Lower limit 5%	Upper limit 5%	Upper limit 1%	n	Lower limit 1%	Lower limit 5%	Upper limit 5%	Upper limit 1%
1					31	7	9	22	24	61	20	22	39	41
2					32	8	9	23	24	62	20	22	40	42
3				3	33	8	10	23	25	63	20	23	40	43
4				4	34	9	10	24	25	64	21	23	41	43
5			5	5	35	9	11	24	26	65	21	24	41	44
6		0	6	6	36	9	11	25	27	66	22	24	42	44
7		0	7	7	37	10	12	25	27	67	22	25	42	45
8	0	0	8	8	38	10	12	26	28	68	22	25	43	46
9	0	1	8	9	39	11	12	27	28	69	23	25	44	46
10	0	1	9	10	40	11	13	27	29	70	23	26	44	47
11	0	1	10	11	41	11	13	28	30	71	24	26	45	47
12	1	2	10	11	42	12	14	28	30	72	24	27	45	48
13	1	2	11	12	43	12	14	29	31	73	25	27	46	48
14	1	2	12	13	44	13	15	29	31	74	25	28	46	49
15	2	3	12	13	45	13	15	30	32	75	25	28	47	50
16	2	3	13	14	46	13	15	31	33	76	26	28	48	50
17	2	4	13	15	47	14	16	31	33	77	26	29	48	51
18	3	4	14	15	48	14	16	32	34	78	27	29	49	51
19	3	4	15	16	49	15	17	32	34	79	27	30	49	52
20	3	5	15	17	50	15	17	33	35	80	28	30	50	52
21	4	5	16	17	51	15	18	33	36	81	28	31	50	53
22	4	5	17	18	52	16	18	34	36	82	28	31	51	54
23	4	6	17	19	53	16	18	35	37	83	29	32	51	54
24	5	6	18	19	54	17	19	35	37	84	29	32	52	55
25	5	7	18	20	55	17	19	36	38	85	30	32	53	55
26	6	7	19	20	56	17	20	36	39	86	30	33	53	56
27	6	7	20	21	57	18	20	37	39	87	31	33	54	56
28	6	8	20	22	58	18	21	37	40	88	31	34	54	57
29	7	8	21	22	59	19	21	38	40	89	31	34	55	58
30	7	9	21	23	60	19	21	39	41	90	32	35	55	58

Appendix II: α and R scales for binomial probability papers

σ scale

To prepare the α and R scales, we must first determine the σ scale (population standard deviation). Let 5mm correspond to 1σ in binomial probability papers so that the σ scale is graduated every 5mm as 1σ. When the scale factor of 1/10 is selected, it is graduated every $5/\sqrt{10} = 1.58$ mm as 1σ.

α scale

The α scale can be obtained from table 1 below. When the scale factor of 1/10 is selected, each value should be multiplied by $1/\sqrt{10}$.

Table 1 α scale and $1/\sqrt{10}$ α scale

Probability		Length of scale		
Single side	Both sides	0	α scale (cm)	$1/\sqrt{10} - \alpha$ (cm)
0.25	0.50	0.67	0.34	0.11
0.10	0.20	1.28	0.64	0.20
0.05	0.10	1.64	0.82	0.26
0.025	0.05	1.96	0.98	0.31
0.010	0.02	2.33	1.16	0.37
0.005	0.01	2.58	1.29	0.41
0.001	0.002	3.09	1.54	0.49
0.0005	0.001	3.29	1.64	0.52

R scale

Let R be the range of a sample of size n drawn from a normal population whose variance is σ^2. Find the value c, such that the probability of R being greater than $c\sigma$ is equal to 0.05 or 0.01. This c is multiplied by 5mm equivalent to 1σ in the binomial probability paper to obtain the R scale. Corresponding R values for various sample sizes and probabilities are shown in table 2.

Table 2 R scale

	Probability 0.05		Probability 0.01	
Sample size	σ	R Scale (cm)	σ	R Scale (cm)
2	2.77	1.38	3.64	1.82
3	3.31	1.66	4.12	2.06
4	3.63	1.82	4.40	2.20
5	3.86	1.93	4.60	2.30
6	4.03	2.02	4.76	2.38
7	4.17	2.08	4.88	2.44
8	4.29	2.14	4.99	2.50
9	4.39	2.20	5.08	2.54
10	4.47	2.24	5.16	2.58
15	4.80	2.40	5.45	2.72
20	5.01	2.50	5.65	2.82

Bibliography

1. American Military Standards
2. ASTM Manual on Quality Control of Materials, 1951
3. Burr, Irving W., Engineering Statistics and Quality Control, McGraw-Hill Book Company, Inc., New York, 1953
4. Columbia University, Statistical Research Group, Selected Techniques of Statistical Analysis, McGraw-Hill, 1947
5. Duncan, A.J., Industrial Quality Control, 1950
6. Ferrel, E.B., Industrial Quality Control, 1953
7. Juran, J.M., Quality Control Handbook, McGraw-Hill Book Company, Inc., New York
8. Merrington, M. and Thompson, C.M., Biometrika, 1943
9. Mosteller, F., Turkey, J.W., Binomial Probability Paper, Codex Book Co., Inc., Norwood, Mass., 1946
10. Pearson, E.S. and Hartley, H.O., Biometrika Tables for Statisticians, Vol. I., Cambridge University Press, 1954
11. Thompson, C.M., Biometrika, 1941-2
12. Tukey, J.W., ASQC Conference Papers, 1951
13. Welch, B.L., Biometrika, 1954

Index